real
influencing

real
influencing

how to win hearts
and minds to
achieve goals

JK SMART

PEARSON

Prentice Hall

BUSINESS

London • New York • Toronto • Sydney • Tokyo • Singapore
Hong Kong • Cape Town • Madrid • Paris • Amsterdam • Munich • Milan

PEARSON EDUCATION LIMITED

Head Office:
Edinburgh Gate
Harlow CM20 2JE
Tel: +44 (0)1279 623623
Fax: +44 (0)1279 431059

Website: www.pearsoned.co.uk

First published in Great Britain in 2003

© Pearson Education Limited 2003

The right of JK Smart to be identified as author of this work has been asserted
by her in accordance with the Copyright, Designs and Patents Act 1988.

ISBN 0 273 66329 1

British Library Cataloguing in Publication Data
A CIP catalogue record for this book can be obtained from the British Library

10 9 8 7 6 5 4 3 2 1

Designed by Claire Brodmann Book Designs, Lichfield, Staffs
Typeset by Northern Phototypesetting Co. Ltd, Bolton
Printed and bound in Great Britain by Bell & Bain Ltd, Glasgow

The Publishers' policy is to use paper manufactured from sustainable forests.

To my beloved grandmother,
my first formative influence,
still sorely missed.

With thanks to all the people who once had a
formative influence (especially Paul, Fiona, Allan
and Maxine who helped me discover my principles)
and to Sharleen Spitteri and Texas for providing
the soundtrack to the writing.

Contents

PART 2
Getting influencing right in the *real* world

PART 3
Knowing when you need to adjust your approach 105

Conclusion 141

Appendix 147

About the author

Karen Smart's background is in individual and organizational development. However, unlike some in her field, first and foremost Karen sees herself as a line manager. In recent years, she's worked primarily on enabling managers to manage – developing and delivering everything from individual skill building and management development programmes to management systems design and organization wide culture change. In addition to managing her team, Karen has coached senior managers and facilitated cross-functional working, problem solving and conflict management. Although she has two degrees and has researched extensively across a range of disciplines, ultimately Karen feels she's learned most about management from her experience as an overworked and undervalued manager, disempowered by bureaucracy. From this experience – and inspired by the man she says 'puts the J into JK Smart and a lot of the smart too' – the philosophy of *real* management for *real* people was born.

■ *real* management for the way it is ■

Introduction to *real* management

▶ Welcome to the *real* world

Do you read most management books and say, 'If only it was that easy in the real world'? *Real* management is the answer for every manager who knows it's about doing the best we can with what we've got, in the real world of organizations that are demanding more and more for less and less. It's for real managers who think the books we've read must have been written by people who don't live in our world and who mistake us for superheroes. We know we could work out a better way of managing if only we could get off the treadmill long enough to find the time.

▶ Telling it like it is

But what if someone had read everything, tried everything, worked out why things don't work in the real world, found a way of managing that works with the complexity of real life instead of pretending it's simple, and then taken time off from managing to tell you about it? And what if that someone wasn't a guru, academic or consultant but an ordinary, overworked manager who knows what managers are up against and who doesn't judge or preach or try to get people to be something they're not? And what if that same manager understood that the idea of 'one size fits all' doesn't work and offered you a way of blending her insight with your experience so you could become the manager you were meant to be?

Real **management:**

■ Makes sense of your experience by explaining why, when we do things by the book, they don't work.

■ Is based on a common-sense understanding of human nature that takes your concerns seriously and starts from the assumption that what you're doing now makes sense for the situation you're in.

■ Helps you turn your past experience into the key that unlocks your best ever management performance.

1

Confessions of an overworked manager

Towards a new way of managing in the *real* world

I'm tired of being overworked – are you?

I'm not a management guru. I'm an overworked manager who got sick of being overworked. I love my work so I give it 100 per cent . . . I push my team . . . we achieve things . . . I'm given more work . . . I give it 110 per cent . . . I push my team a bit harder . . . we achieve more things . . . I'm given more work . . . need I go on? Stress researchers say our automatic response to overload is to do what we were doing before only harder and for longer. Psychologists say insanity is doing the same things over and over and expecting different results. So, as they say in America, 'You do the math!'

There has to be a better way of working

Psychologists also say that if you want a different result, you have to do something different. Since I started my management career, I've seen (and been guilty of) the sorry way managers treat their staff (and vice versa), and I've become increasingly disillusioned with the established wisdom about managing people. I began to believe there had to be a better way.

> **Beliefs** are thoughts we use to guide our decisions and actions, although we tend to forget and see them as indisputable facts. With any action, a belief always comes first. We find evidence to support our beliefs in our experience. Once we've got a belief, we tend not to question it, unless an experience forces us to.

People shouldn't have to leave their brains at the door or become robots when they come into work. They shouldn't have to run ever harder just to stand still. In recent years, I've watched people go sick with stress and I've seen stress-management programmes being offered as the cure, all the time thinking that we must be in big trouble if we're settling for *managing* stress instead of removing it at source. I knew there had to be a way to remove the stress caused by the gap between who we are outside of work and who we have to be at work. There had to be a way of managing that isn't soul-destroying for everyone involved. I just didn't know what that way was. Then I met someone who changed the way I think about people; who motivated me to find a new way of managing; who influenced me to want to be a better manager; and who inspired me to take time out and write this series of books in the hope that I could do for others what he did for me.

There had to be a way of managing that isn't soul-destroying for everyone involved.

Getting out of the box of traditional management thinking

I started as a management trainee on a year's development programme, during which I became fascinated by the way people manage, and I've been a student of management as well as a manager ever since. I'm exaggerating (but, sadly, only slightly) when I say that by the time I decided there had to be a better way, I'd already read and tried everything ever published about management. Clearly, if I wanted new answers I had to look in new places. Not one to do things by halves, I've looked close to management, in neuroscience, psychology and psychotherapy to learn how our brains work, why we do the things we do, and how to deal with emotions and the effects of early conditioning on our behaviour. And I've looked far from management – everything from aikido to Zen Buddhism via horticulture and homoeopathy (well, if we aren't growing something as managers, we're curing it, right?). And yes, I confess, I've read almost everything the self-help movement has to offer, sifting the sensible from the senseless.

Looking for what makes sense

After years of being a task-focused manager working for organizations in 'initiative' mode, I can assure you I'm too sceptical about the 'next new idea' and the 'one size fits all' solution to have bought into any one set of beliefs. Instead, what I've done is collect and use the ideas that made sense of my experience. Small sentence, big idea, so let me say it again. I researched a wide range of subjects and whenever I got a feeling of 'that's obvious', I applied the idea to the way I manage and used my experience to figure out what worked.

> **Trial and error** is how we learn from experience – trying to do something, noticing what doesn't work, and changing our approach until we find what works. More often than not, we decide what works and doesn't work based on the feedback we get.

I want to make it easier for you than it was for me

It would be hypocritical for me to tell you I'm sceptical of people who sell you the 'one right way' and then try to do the same thing myself, so that's not what I'm doing. I'm sharing what I've learned to save you having to do all the research I did. But I can't do it all for you – we have to be in it together.

Equal partners or no deal

Ninety-five per cent of what we learn comes from experience, with only five per cent coming from books, training, etc., and they only work when they resonate with our own experience by triggering memories of earlier experiences.

> We have vast quantities of experience that we can't hold in our **conscious minds** so we store these experiences in our subconscious. The trouble with our **subconscious** is that it's sub (below) conscious (the level of our awareness) so we aren't conscious of (don't know) what's in there. We need triggers to surface it.

A good book is, in effect, telling you something you already know intuitively; you just haven't articulated it on a conscious level.

> **Intuition** is that feeling of knowing something, without knowing how you know it. It means you're using information from your subconscious mind that your conscious mind isn't aware of.

What I'm telling you will work only if you use my insight as a trigger for surfacing your experience and intuitive (subconscious) insight because, in the end, only your insight can improve your performance. It's 'equal partnership learning' – I provide the trigger, you provide the experience. I have no ambition to create clones of me. I want people to manage in a way that works for them – a way that suits their unique blend of insight and experience. What I *am* hoping for, though, is that you'll think what I'm saying is common sense.

> **Common sense** (a rarity in life) is when something is both logical (appealing to our conscious minds) and intuitive (appealing to our subconscious minds) and we get a 'that's obvious' feeling. When our conscious and subconscious minds are out of sync, we get an 'off' feeling – something isn't quite right, but we don't know why.

So, as you read this book, think about your experience and see if you get a 'that's obvious' feeling. If you do, then try my approach, learn from it, and adapt it to meet your needs. If you get an 'off' feeling, then challenge what I'm saying, come to your own insight, try that, learn from it, and adapt it to meet your needs.

Starting from where people are

The biggest mistake people make when trying to help move someone forward is to assume they're both starting from the same place – something that never happens in real life. I don't want to make that mistake with you, so throughout this book – in shaded boxes – I explain the concepts and beliefs that underpin my approach to management. In the Appendix, there's also a broader look at where I'm coming from as a manager.

Let's keep it real here

If you're like most managers I know, you won't have time to read a heavyweight volume (even if I had time to write one), but you won't want to be fobbed off with one-minute answers that only work in books either. So what I've done (to give you the best of both worlds) is to put some powerful messages – that hopefully will resonate with your own experience and trigger your insight – into a quick but intense read. There's also a reminder of the key messages and some questions to think about at the end of each chapter.

Let me know what you think

I mean what I say about being equal partners, so if you want to share your experience and insight or ask questions about anything in the book, I'd really like to hear from you. You can email me at **JKSmartBooks@aol.com**. I take on a few telephone coaching clients each year so managers who are interested may email me as may trainers and development specialists who are interested in attending an 'equal partners learning programme' to be licensed to work with this material.

IN SHORT

▶ We can't keep doing what we've always been doing because it doesn't work and it stresses us out in the process.

▶ People who still tout the established management wisdom are 'flat earthers' who need to be challenged to develop an approach that works in the real world.

▶ I'm not telling you anything you don't already know: I'm only helping you to bring your insight to the surface where you can do something with it.

▶ Challenge everything I say, and take away only what makes sense of your experience.

2

The key to unlocking your best ever performance

Track back from your experience, then work forward from your beliefs

We already have everything we need to be effective

We just have preferences for, and are more skilled in, some things than others (a result of them being our preferences). Development, especially in people skills, isn't about teaching new skills as much as about unblocking existing ones. What blocks our development? Our beliefs, which govern how we use our characteristics. Lack of self-belief is the single biggest block to excellent performance. Once you get that sorted, everything else falls into place.

But our beliefs hinder us from using them

You may have excellent communication skills, but if you believe that talking never solved anything, then they're not likely to get much of an outing, so how will you ever know just how good they are? Have you ever thought, 'I wish I could do that but I'm not confident/bright/calm/etc. enough'? What are the component parts of the skill you wish you had? Do you use them in any other activity or part of your life?

And so do our judgements about ourselves

What's your biggest strength? Okay, in what kinds of situations does it really help you to perform well? Now identify at least one situation in which it hinders your performance. You may find this hard, but persevere, because I guarantee there will be at least one. If in doubt, ask a trusted colleague. Now, relabel the strength as a neutral word or phrase that would apply equally to both the helpful and hindering situations. When you've done that, try the same exercise again but this time for your biggest weakness and, suddenly, we don't have strengths and weaknesses any more; we have characteristics.

> A **characteristic** is a piece of knowledge, an attitude, a behaviour, a skill, or any single input you bring to your performance. It is described neutrally to avoid implying strength or weakness. For example, I'm not lazy, I'm someone who doesn't like to waste energy. The same characteristic can be helpful or hindering depending on the context in which it is used.

The need to find and challenge our hindering beliefs

Are you happy with your results in all areas of your life? People are happy with their performance when the external world matches their inner reality and unhappy when it doesn't.

> My definition of **sanity** is when the external world matches the picture of it that we have in our minds without us having to distort either what's out there or what's in our minds. It's when we see things as they are, not as we wish they were.

There are people who are happy or unhappy for healthy reasons (they see things as they really are and not as they'd like them to be). There are also people who are happy (but delusional) or unhappy (but victims) for unhealthy reasons (they distort what they see to conform to their inner reality).

> Our **subconscious creates experiences** for us (from events) that reinforce what we believe about the world and the people in it, if necessary by distorting the picture so we see only what we want to see. But, while it does this to keep us feeling sane on a day-to-day basis (yes, even when all around us think we're delusional), it craftily creates negative experiences when it wants to push us into re-examining our beliefs. And if we don't re-examine our beliefs after a negative experience, it keeps recreating the same experience until we give in and do what it wants.

Effectiveness is when people are happy for healthy reasons. If you're not happy with the responses you're getting and the experiences you're creating, then you have three choices:

1. Carry on as you are, a victim in your own melodrama, blaming circumstances or other people and dragging the rest of us down with you.

2. Reframe the results so that you turn them into a positive experience that you can be happy about.

> **Reframing** is when we change our interpretation of an event, usually by challenging the beliefs that underpin our original interpretation. We do this by finding other ways of looking at it.

3. Assume what you got was what you wanted and track back to the beliefs that drove the behaviour. If you're okay with the beliefs, then go back to option 2. If you're not, then re-examine them and develop alternatives to change your behaviour and achieve different results.

We all know how to do option 1 but what about the rest? Easier said than done? Yes, if you associate change with behaviour change, but I'm talking about belief changes that take milliseconds to achieve and last forever and – and this is the big plus – a changed belief triggers a changed behaviour in ways that don't require mountains of will-power to sustain. Want to give it a try? Read on . . .

A changed belief triggers a changed behaviour without requiring mountains of willpower.

IN SHORT

♦ You've got everything you need already; it's only your beliefs that are holding you back.

♦ Stop being so hard on yourself: being judgemental and self-critical never helped anyone improve.

♦ Take the acid test: ask yourself if you're happy with the results that you are achieving.

▶ If you're not happy, don't just sit there; do something about it.

3

If it's as easy as the books make out, why are there so many books?

Resisting the temptation to want easy answers in a complex world

It's not my fault – it's the way I'm programmed

It's scientific fact, mother! Wanting easy answers doesn't make me lazy. Brains are hard-wired to lay down programmes in our subconscious so we can do things without thinking (on autopilot, if you like), leaving us with plenty of spare capacity to deal with the unexpected.

> The brain develops **programmes** in our subconscious, based on our experiences. When it registers an unfamiliar event, it quickly (so quickly we don't know it's happening) looks for a suitable pre-existing programme (**pre-programme** for short) to interpret the event (like a computer matching fingerprints). When it registers a good enough match, it automatically triggers the response from the earlier experience.

Trainers call the pre-programmes that serve us well 'unconscious competence'.

At the bottom of the learning ladder is **unconscious incompetence** (when we don't know what we don't know), then **conscious incompetence** (when we realize we need to learn something), followed by **conscious competence** (when we're mastering a skill and still have to concentrate all the time we're doing it). This stage continues until we can do it without having to think (**unconscious competence**). Driving is the classic example.

So many choices – so little time

The trouble with being an overworked manager is that the only time I get a taste of the huge variety today's world has to offer is when I'm skimming the Sunday papers, and let's face it, who has time to do more than skim when there's so many sections? I used to like that line in Kipling's *If* about filling the unforgiving minute with 60 seconds' worth of distance run . . . until I had to live it! Ignoring the fact that some of today's time-saving devices don't actually do what they say on the tin (I'd mention email, but don't get me started on that or we'll be here all day), it's the ever increasing expectations of what we're meant to do with the time we save that get me. It's as though if we're not working flat out to improve the quality of our relationships, bodies, spirits and lifestyles – and don't forget careers – then we're somehow failing to make the most of everything that twenty-first-century life has to offer.

Is it any surprise that, as managers, we want one-minute answers to twenty-year problems? Who has time to spend with their staff these days, when the pressure to deliver more outputs with fewer resources is greater than ever? No wonder hypocrisy creeps in, as on a recent appraisal training course, where a group of management-level appraisees had no problem saying that for their own appraisal they wanted their manager to take as much time as it needed to do a good job, but that they were far too busy to do that for their team members.

The customer is king – so give them what they want

An IT manager asked me to approve a plan for recruiting IT officers for a number of local offices around the country. He wanted to run the selection process at HQ, with IT experts interviewing and then allocating successful candidates to local managers. He wanted the recruits to have high-quality IT skills, and he knew local managers weren't IT literate enough to ensure that. Something wasn't right with his proposal (my 'off' feeling), so I probed and discovered he feared local managers wouldn't have ownership of the national IT strategy if they'd had no say in the appointment of their IT officer. In the end, we recruited at local level with an IT person doing the shortlist (for quality control) and asking the technical questions, but with the local line manager making the final decision. The solution gave the IT manager everything he needed, which he wouldn't have got if I'd just given him what he wanted.

A lot of organizations buy into the 'customer is king' myth, and so must many management writers, otherwise quick-fix, autopilot, 'one-size-fits-all' solutions wouldn't be so prevalent on the management shelves of your local bookstore. Books that offer solutions that would insult your intelligence if you weren't so distracted by the demands of your job. Solutions that *do* insult your subconscious intelligence if only you had time to listen to it. And when you *do* look beyond the glib answers, what do you find? A complex world overcomplicated by impenetrable academics or the fashionable world of the latest management guru who thinks you can solve everything by applying an alarmingly alliterative acronym!

We need *real* answers for the way it is in the *real* world

Real managers run a mile from formulaic approaches that treat human beings as a constant when they're a variable. We know people make money by giving us what we want regardless of whether it's what we need, but in the *real* world what's important is what works, not what's quick. We need to find a way to meet our conscious need for easy answers with our subconscious need for a common-sense approach that works with the complexity of human nature.

IN SHORT

▶ We may be programmed to want easy answers, but we don't have to give in to temptation.

▶ We have so many choices about how to spend our time that it makes sense not to waste time getting our people management wrong.

▶ What we want isn't always what we need, so we need to think before we buy what's on offer.

▶ Yes, we *want* easy answers, but we *need* answers that
work, so let's not settle for shabby compromise: let's get
the best of both worlds.

PART 1

■ *real* management for the way it is ■

Understanding why influencing goes wrong so you can put it right

▶ **Understanding the cause and effect relationships**

As an overworked manager, I find it easy to get sucked into dealing with things at surface level rather than taking time to do things properly. I get a buzz out of taking decisive action so I find it hard to slow down and make the effort to understand why something has gone wrong, even though I know the buzz won't last!

▶ **Taking a long hard look at the way we influence**

If you're anything like me, you'll be itching to get straight to the 'how to do it' part. But remember, that's where we went wrong in the past, so please bear with me because we can't put something right unless we understand why it went wrong in the first place. In a quick read, I don't have time to give you lots of examples plus my insights so I'm going to explore one big example in depth. I've used a composite of several real-life experiences so I can highlight the issues that undermine our approach to influencing.

4

Why is influencing always about the messenger, not the message?

Insiders, outsiders and being the bearer of bad news

Taking on a hostile team – and organization

> At my interview, they asked how I'd cope with someone working for me who'd applied for the job I'd got. I said I'd do my job, let my work show why I'd been appointed and deal with any problems with that person just as I would with any interpersonal problem.

> It wasn't a hypothetical question. I spent my first few weeks meeting my team and the heads of department who'd be my main customers. I wasn't wanted by either. It was the worst induction I've ever had and most days I went home wishing I'd turned the job down. You may not have experienced the induction from hell, but I'll bet you've taken on a team and had to influence them to work your way rather than your predecessor's. That's what this story is about.

If it ain't broke

The strong message I got from the heads of department was that the organization was very successful as it was, thank you, so it didn't need to change. They quoted statistics about operational performance. They waxed lyrical about the smart way they dealt with problems. They positively swooned about the efficiency of their processes. They said everything in the garden was rosy.

Then I got my first real cultural clue. The head of department I was meeting was called out to see the Chief Executive about a problem in his department that had been leaked to the press. As he left, he grimaced and said 'it's phone book down trousers time again'. I thought 'everything in the garden rosy, is it? Pretty strange roses, if you ask me?'

Bringing bad news – from our customers

As adamant as they were that things in their department were fine, they were equally adamant that things in my own team were not. The criticisms came thick and fast about the way the service had been run under my predecessor (who had been moved sideways but was still around) and, Michael, his direct report (the man who'd applied for my job). They complained about everything from the quality of the courses on offer, the lack of flexibility and variety and the complacent, unresponsive manner of the team. I won't bore you with the detail.

I'm a great believer in open and honest communication in my team so I made a point of telling Michael what had come out of my meetings. I was careful only to report what had been said and not my interpretation or judgement. Michael was upset but didn't comment. I was puzzled about this until my predecessor rang to tell me he knew what had been said and it was the first they'd heard of it. I challenged the heads of departments and they said they hadn't felt giving the feedback would change anything – until my arrival. I was horrified. Michael and his former boss had clearly believed no news is good news. Well, at least it explained Michael's off manner with me because if ever there was a case of 'bad news, shoot the messenger' this was it.

And from my own perspective

Our **perspective** is basically what we see from the position we are looking at things from. Anyone who is in a different position from you [including your team member] is bound to look at things differently. And as our actions are based on our interpretation of what we see and hear, a different perspective will lead to different action.

I didn't just rely on customer feedback. I made my own assessment. I compared the services they were providing with my idea of a first class training team. To be honest, I had a hard time keeping an appalled look off my face because it was the most amateurish set up I've ever seen. But it wasn't the absence of a library of training materials, the archaic use of acetates and old photocopied handouts, the meaningless happy sheets that never got analyzed or the absence of anything other than traditional classroom style training (not surprising considering they hadn't even heard of CDRom training!) that got me. It was the fact that they seemed to pride themselves on their professionalism. It had to be the biggest blindspot I'd seen in years.

The idea of a **blindspot** [the technical term is scotoma] has been borrowed by psychologists from the field of ophthalmology, where it means a situation in which part of a person's visual field just does not work. The person can see everything else, but they can see nothing in the area of the scotoma. And they cannot know what it is they aren't seeing. They are 'blind' to the 'blindspot'. In the field of psychology, it refers to a mental blindspot, where a person is simply unaware of their own role in creating a particular experience.

The dubious pleasure of being an outsider

On my third day in the job, a veteran senior manager had told me that people didn't listen to outsiders here until they'd been there six months. I thought he was exaggerating (as it turned out, he was underestimating), so I decided to use the time to influence my team in new ways of working so they could improve our service and become trailblazers for the new organizational culture I'd been brought in to create.

The upside of being an outsider is that the issues fairly leap out at you. The downside is that the people on the inside won't listen to you when you tell them about it. It's partly because you're an outsider, obviously, but it's more complex than that. It's also to do with the fact that they genuinely don't see what you see. They're not being difficult, they're being controlled by their reticular activating system.

Our **reticular activating system** [RAS] is a brain function that makes us notice things that are significant to us but not notice things that aren't. We need it because there's so much information to process all the time that without it we couldn't function.

Once people have made their minds up about something, they literally don't see anything that doesn't support their judgement.

If at first you don't succeed

After three weeks of intense analysis, I had a pretty clear idea of what had to change but all I'd actually achieved was to alienate people with my feedback. They hadn't listened, which wasn't entirely unexpected. We all have our coping strategies for dealing with criticism and ignoring the person doing the criticizing is a pretty popular one.

A **coping strategy** is a pattern of behaviour that we use repeatedly as a defence against things we fear we can't cope with. They're habits and, like everything else, can be helpful or hindering depending on the situation, the use you make of them and the effect they have.

And why shouldn't they ignore me? *I* knew I was good at my job but they didn't. I needed to establish my credibility with them but how was I going to do that?

IN SHORT

▶ **Be careful the messenger doesn't detract from the message.** Have you ever been shot for being the bringer of bad news?

▶ **Insiders see things differently from outsiders.** What's your experience of the different perspectives of insiders and outsiders?

▶ **Criticism is always personal.** What's your coping strategy?

5

Why did I think rational argument would work?

Starting from where people are, not from where you want them to be

Presenting to impress

If I say so myself, after endless practice, I'm an impressive presenter – a relaxed, confident speaker, at ease with my audience, knowledgeable and passionate about my subject and quick on my feet with questions. Maybe that's why I decided to choose a presentation to unleash the full force of my persuasive powers on the team. I had two aims: cement my credibility as an expert and provide a vision for our service that we could rally behind.

I got the whole team together and gave it everything I had. I emphasized how important a role we'd have in achieving the new culture which I described in loving detail. I was careful not to criticize the current state but I did make a cogent case for change.

But only impressing as a presenter

They listened – some of them even made notes. They were impressed with my presentation skills but not with my ideas.

Michael said it all sounded exciting but he wasn't sure the organization was ready for it. One of the less assertive team members asked about how we'd get the budget to pay for it all and, although her tone of voice was neutral, I sensed an air of cynicism. They asked clarification questions so by the end of the meeting I felt they understood what I was saying but they weren't interested. I got the message as clearly as if they'd said 'thanks, but no thanks'.

One person's rational argument is another person's madness

At home that evening, I did a review for learning on my own.

> I regularly do reviews for learning with my team – sometimes one to one and sometimes with a whole project group, depending on the issue. We prepare by considering the following questions first on our own and then together.
>
> - What went well and less well? What did I do to contribute to the outcome? What do I know now that I didn't know before?
> - What have I learned about my own behaviour [about myself, the way other people behave, etc.]? What insight have I gained about dealing with this kind of experience in the future?
> - To enable me to use what I have learned what, if anything, do I need to challenge about the way I think or the way I behave? Are there any old ideas or behaviours I need to unlearn first?
> - How, where and when can I use this insight to improve my performance?

I learned that my reasoning hadn't made sense to them. I knew we each make sense of our world by using our beliefs to interpret events to create our experience and, because everyone's belief system is different, the sense they make of the same situation will be different. So, clearly, they didn't share my beliefs on training and culture change.

Experience = event + interpretation

Very little of what we call our experience is things that happen to us [events]. Most of it is about how we interpret [make sense of] those events.

I also learned there was a lot more than rational argument going on here. I was proposing to change the very current state that these people had created. They felt ownership of the very service I was implying wasn't what the organization needed.

Finding their logic

Although I still felt my diagnosis and proposals were right, I accepted they didn't. If I was going to influence them round to my way of thinking, I had to find their logic.

I use the term **'logic'** to mean our unique concept of rational cause and effect. Everyone has their own logic, so if you work backwards from the effects people achieve and ask yourself why someone would want to do that you will find the belief that caused them to produce that effect – that's their logic.

And working with it instead of trying to impose mine

As a manager who'd spent most of my career working at a strategic level my natural way of working is to focus on where I want to be and on the gap between that and where I am. And that *is* important, but it needs to be balanced by a recognition that when dealing with people you have to start from where they are. I needed to find out where that was which meant it was going to take longer than I thought to win them round.

And I still had an organizational culture to change. I reread my notes on my initial meetings with the heads of departments and found one man (head of the marketing department) who'd hinted at a couple of areas of dissatisfaction. I decided to see if there was anything I could do to help.

IN SHORT

▶ **It takes more than knowing your stuff to influence people.** What do you rely on most when it comes to influencing people?

▶ **Rational argument only works with people who share your logic.** What's your worst experience of failing to win the argument?

▶ **Start from where *people* are, not from where *you* are.** Do you adjust your proposals to take account of the views of the people you're trying to influence?

6

Why do I waste my time trying to win people round?

Shifting from 'push' to 'pull' and influencing by 'being'

Going back to basics

I realized how much influence Michael had with the rest of my team so I spent a lot of time with him. I found the things that frustrated him – like not having enough money to buy good-quality training resources – and did something about them. I developed a 'both/and' approach – which meant blending the best of the either/or options – which was reactive and proactive at the same time. Reactive in the sense of not imposing myself on people but waiting for them to come to me with their problems (though I did put myself about a lot, reminding people I was there to help if needed) and proactive in making sure I helped in ways that moved my agenda forward too.

And letting my work speak for itself

I also stopped *trying* to impress people. Instead, I did what I'd said I'd do in the interview – let my work speak for me. My first priority as a manager was to raise my team's game. If we were going to be at the forefront of major culture change, we needed to set an example for others. Also, I wanted to demonstrate to my fellow senior managers that if I could change the culture in my team, they could do the same in theirs. And, yes, I admit I wanted them to see that I could practise as well as preach.

Raising other people's standards is a fool's game

As anyone who's tried to turn round a poorly performing team will know, it's a hard, often demoralizing, and usually thankless task. I wouldn't say I've got a great desire to be liked (respected – now, that's a different story) but I don't like being the bad guy. Still, it had to be done so whenever I was given a piece of work that wasn't good enough, I gave it back, along with my analysis of their performance and coaching on how they could improve. I was like a dripping tap because, if I let up for even a minute, they slipped back into their old sloppy ways. Nothing left the team until I'd cleared it – most days my in-tray looked like the Leaning Tower of Pisa!

Because only they can do it for themselves

Of course, it didn't work and I eventually worked out why.

We all have an **internal regulator** that maintains our standards at the level our subconscious thinks is right for us, based on our beliefs about ourselves. Its job is to pull us up to our standard when we slip back and to drag us back when we get above ourselves. If we don't think highly of ourselves, we settle for lower standards than we're capable of, or we push ourselves to achieve perfection – either way we feel bad about ourselves. We can't change our internal regulator until we change our beliefs about ourselves.

I needed to find a way of getting them to want to raise their own standards. And that clearly meant influencing their beliefs about themselves.

From 'push' to 'pull'

You've heard the old joke. How many psychologists does it take to change a light bulb? One but the light bulb has to want to change. Well, many a true word spoken in jest is all I can say. You can't influence people who don't want to be influenced. I took a different tack. I stopped trying to persuade them and started telling them stories about my experience of being part of a highly valued team making a crucial contribution. I worked one to one with key team members, finding out what mattered most to them, what gave them job satisfaction, the one thing they'd change about the culture if they could. Instead of analyzing their performance, I facilitated their analyzing their own performance. When they talked about strengths and weaknesses, I talked about characteristics that are sometimes helpful and sometimes hindering.

Slowly they stopped thinking small and started expanding their horizons. Slowly they started to see they had potential to do better work and make a bigger impact. I made sure they got the credit whenever they did good work. And in the same plain unvarnished way I'd given them the original negative feedback, I gave them the positive feedback that had started to come back from our customers.

Being myself, warts and all

One incident stands out in my mind from that time. Michael was recruiting a junior manager and I asked to see the application forms of the candidates he'd shortlisted. As I read them, I noted the questions that came into my head. As I gave them back, I said I'd found the forms fascinating reading and I'd be interested in getting his feedback from the interviews on the questions I'd raised.

I went back to my office and shortly afterwards Michael stormed in. He was livid, demanding to know if I thought he wasn't capable of doing the recruitment. It was obviously a rhetorical question as he clearly believed I didn't rate him. I was taken aback by his manner but, more than anything, I was surprised at his interpretation because that thought had never occurred to me. I felt an answering anger rise in me which is maybe why I didn't stop and give a considered response. I looked him straight in the eye and said, 'Michael, if I hadn't been happy for you to do the recruitment, you wouldn't be doing it.' It was clear from the stunned look on his face that he was finding it hard to square his belief that I didn't rate him with his belief that I was being sincere in my reply. To his credit, his cognitive dissonance didn't last long.

Cognitive dissonance happens when we try to hold two opposing thoughts at the same time. The mind can't cope with it, so works hard to get rid of the inconsistency [dissonance] in one of three ways:

1. By reducing the importance of the dissonant beliefs.
2. By increasing the number of consistent beliefs to outweigh the dissonant ones.
3. By reinterpreting the dissonant beliefs so they're no longer inconsistent.

I know a smoker who uses all three!

It's our congruence that influences people

Analyzing it later, I think it was the speed of my reply combined with the look of puzzlement on my face at his accusation that convinced him. All the feedback he'd picked up from my reaction must have told him the same thing – that I was sincere.

By **feedback**, I mean any signs we pick up about reactions to what we're doing. It's not just the formal feedback we get when the boss reviews our work, it's all the little signals we don't necessarily notice consciously but that our subconscious mind picks up and uses to adjust our thinking, behaviour and actions. We get feedback all the time regardless of whether we think we do. Without it, we'd never know how to adjust course to achieve our intentions.

I didn't realize it at the time but it was a turning point in our relationship. After that he trusted me. And looking back, I think that must have been the point at which I realized that it's not the big things we do that influence people, it's the way we are in our everyday, unconscious moments of choice.

IN SHORT

> **Less 'push', more 'pull'.** If I asked your team, would they say you were more 'push' or 'pull'?

> **Don't play games, be yourself.** How often do you get to be yourself at work and how often are you playing a role?

> **We influence people most when we are congruent.** Who has influenced you most and are they congruent?

7

Why do people wish they'd listened when its too late?

It's not *your* insight that influences them, it's theirs

Getting a sense of déjà vu

As word got round about our improving quality, we got more requests to work with managers. We made a lot of progress using the reactive/proactive strategy, but along the way I was picking up signs of a strange trend. Let me give you some examples.

I desperately wanted to change the level of computer literacy in the team. If everyone could compose handouts straight into a Word document (instead of sending handwritten drafts backwards and forwards to the typing pool), we could improve the quality of our written materials which would in turn improve the professionalism of our image. I couldn't convince the team, who thought I was suggesting they all became typists, but I pulled rank and they complied (definitely a case of exerting power rather than influence) albeit I got more outcomes than the ones I'd bargained for.

We produce **outputs** [things] to achieve **outcomes** [results]. The trouble is, we're often so focused on the outputs that we lose sight of the outcomes yet we exist to deliver outcomes not outputs. There are always more outcomes than you think and many are unintended. For example, if you're working with partners to develop a new product/service, there'll be an outcome about the quality of your relationship and, if you don't pay attention, it might not be an outcome you want.

As I predicted, they quickly got to a point where they couldn't manage without being computer literate. They didn't see it for themselves though, they were too busy revolutionizing our library of training materials. The day they finally saw it was the day Michael came in and, with a sheepish look on his face, told me he was buying a scanner because we couldn't manage without one. We were both smiling as I said 'I told you so'.

Then there was the head of department who came back to me a year after saying his people were too busy to implement appraisal to ask if I could do it now. He told me he wished he'd listened to me a year earlier as it would all be done and dusted by now. He was a customer so I didn't remind him that I'd told him at the time that if he didn't implement it then, he'd regret it later when the pace of change picked up even more.

As someone whose job depends on influencing people, I needed to understand why they didn't listen to me until it was too late. Unexpectedly, I got my answer when coaching a particularly stubborn senior manager.

People only learn from *their* insight, not yours

It was one of the most frustrating yet valuable experiences I've had. Periodically, I'd meet up with the senior manager in question to talk about his recent work experience. He'd talk and I'd listen for anything that didn't make sense to me but that clearly made sense to him – and ask questions. Often my questions would help him reinterpret his experience and I often felt like I was influencing him. But when this had happened several times without any change in his performance, I began to think I wasn't influencing him at all. Then one day, he told me about an experience he'd had that confirmed what we'd been talking about several weeks earlier.

And their insight comes from their experience

From the way he described that experience, I could see that my questions had changed his thinking on a surface or conscious level but it wasn't until he actually experienced what I'd been talking about, that he took it on board at belief (subconscious) level. So, influencing people required change on a conscious and subconscious level.

Which sometimes they have to gain the hard way

The other turning point that happened around that time was my decision to go public with my culture change strategy. We were winning some key people round and carrying out all sorts of useful pilot programmes but we weren't getting the breadth and depth of coverage we needed. I worked with a trusted colleague on a report describing the issues and setting out a broad strategy for culture change. It was a long report but with good reason – we worked in an organization where people were unable to handle the increasing pace of change because they were used to having everything dumbed-down for them by the corporate centre and told what to do. I felt the report needed to be congruent with the cultural values it represented and that meant explaining the complexity of culture change and the reasoning behind the proposals. My thinking was that if we just gave people a list of things to do, it may well be easier for them to read but we'd be implementing the new culture in the style of the old culture – and how pointless is that? My boss disagreed.

Have you seen George Bernard Shaw's quote about there being two great tragedies in life, one is not to get your heart's desire and the other is to get it? Sometimes the only way someone will realize that what they think they want isn't what they really want is for them to get what they think they want and find out for themselves. Well, my boss got what she wanted – a chopped-down overview version of the report with a series of smaller single-subject reports to follow. I knew I couldn't influence her so I just had to accept that if I was right, she would find out for herself soon enough and if I was wrong, well . . . as long as the culture change was successful, all's well that ends well. She never admitted she'd been wrong, but I was with her some months later when her colleagues told her it would have been easier to understand the strategy if we'd had one big report instead of lots of little ones. It was a moment to savour.

But you can influence their experience

I wanted my team to be innovative and take risks instead of playing it safe but I knew their fear of the organization's blame-culture was preventing them. So, I influenced them indirectly by creating a non-blame-culture experience to address their fear and challenge their thinking. I didn't blame people myself and I told them stories of how I dealt with people who tried to blame me. I created a responsibility culture instead that enabled people to make amends for their mistakes and feel good about themselves in the process.

I like the definition of **responsibility** that describes it as **'response-ability'**. Being responsible means that in our moments of choice, we recognize that we don't just have to react, we can respond. It means looking at our options for responding, weighing up the potential consequences of each option, deciding which one will achieve the best results and responding on that basis.

They became more innovative and I learned something else about the skill of influencing.

IN SHORT

▶ **People have to get their own insight.** Have you ever had people come back to you later and say they wished they'd listened?

▶ **Sometimes you have to lose the battle to win the war.** Have you ever given someone what they wanted only for them to find it wasn't what they wanted after all?

▶ **We can influence people's experience.** Have you ever tried to influence someone indirectly by creating a different experience of you for them?

8

Why do you need the patience of a saint for *real* influencing?

Real influencing comes through our relationships and they take time to build

Small steps to a big change

Sometimes, when we take small, imperceptible steps, we don't realize how far we've come until we look back at where we once were. It was like that with my efforts to influence my team (and the wider organizational culture). To be honest, I don't think there was a day when I thought, that's it, I've finally won hearts and minds but I *can* remember the day I realized I'd long since stopped thinking it was an issue.

Real influence is when people are different when you're not there

We were ready to introduce a performance management strategy. The plan was (okay, the Chief Executive's instruction was) that I would talk to senior managers in their departmental groups about the system we used in our team (because they'd be designing their own systems to suit their needs but ours would be the model). When I told my team this, a couple of them asked if they could go in my place and I agreed.

After they got back, they debriefed me on the key points and the interesting stories so it came as a surprise to me when a couple of senior managers rang to tell me something they'd left out. They said my staff had told them how much they got out of being performance managed by me and that they were a great advert for the system. Now, I'm as sceptical as the next man but it was clear that their sincerity had convinced the people who were giving me the feedback.

Playing the long game

There was still a long way to go – in any team some people are tougher to win over than others – but I'd influenced enough people for it to have started spreading to the people with whom they had influence. I knew, because some team members needed emotional support through changes that were deeply personal, that getting them signed up wasn't all there was to it, by any means.

And learning that influencing really is two-way

It wasn't just me who influenced my team, my relationships with them influenced me too. I realized that, the time Michael and I were in a meeting with a manager who'd just joined the organization, discussing a challenging problem that had been going on for years. She was new, enthusiastic and thought it was going to be easy and I found myself explaining why it wasn't. It wasn't until afterwards that I realized how much like Michael I sounded and how much of his thinking I'd made my own. Do you remember how after the first few tortured weeks I changed my approach with Michael? My intention had been to win him over but somewhere along the line we had won each other over and developed an approach to culture change that reflected the best of both of our thinking. And by the time I left, I thought of Michael as the best direct report I'd ever had.

Harnessing the power of stories

In telling you of my efforts to influence my team I've cut a long story short and, in doing so, I may not have given due credit to the power of stories. I used stories all the time to influence people. I told lots of stories about my dealings with the Chief Executive – about his sense of humour and his human side – in an attempt to counter the stories of him being an ogre (which wasn't my experience of him at all). Stories are a great friend to the would-be influencer. It's from the stories that circulate in an organization, even the myths and legends, that people learn the workplace cultural norms. And stories have been used to influence people's thinking since the days of Aesop's fables. It's a basic feature of our memories that we remember best the things that have a story attached.

And stories work both ways for the influencer. Encouraging people to tell their stories gives you a brilliant insight into their character, beliefs and issue. As long as they tell you in narrative-rich form, of course.

Stories are a great friend to the would-be influencer.

Narrative-rich discussions are where you basically get someone to tell you the whole story of the event. If they give you the little details, the nuances, their feelings [all the story's local colour] you can learn so much more about what's happening than you can with a 'just give me the hard facts' approach.

You have to encourage people to do this (asking questions helps) because in the pressure of today's working world, they're bound to be used to keeping it short.

IN SHORT

▶ **Small steps mount up to big changes.** Have you ever looked back to recognize you've come a lot further than you realized?

▶ **Real influence is two-way and shows itself whether you're there or not.** What's your experience of real two-way influencing?

▶ **Harness the power of stories.** In what ways do your stories influence people?

9

Why, even when I do everything right, does it still go wrong?

Because we're human beings, not robots – thank goodness!

What I learned from my influencing experience

I learned that if I hadn't tried to impose my views on people I wouldn't have had so much ground to make up. And if I'd listened as much as I talked, I'd have built relationships with people that provided a good foundation for influencing on specific issues. And if I'd been open to being influenced myself, I'd have had a lot more impact.

Asking the tough questions

If we don't get the results we want, we have to face the possibility that we wanted our influencing attempts to fail. If so, we need to accept that, no matter how much we know logically (consciously) that we need to be more influential, our subconscious wants something else more. And whatever it is, our subconscious will sabotage our efforts until we resolve the discrepancy. If your influencing attempts haven't worked as you would have liked, it may be because you fell into some of the same traps as I did but before you start changing your approach, it's worth checking to see if you really do want to influence – by asking yourself . . .

What do I gain when influencing goes wrong?

Do you worry that if you influence someone and it turns out badly that you'll feel responsible or get blamed? Is it easier to stay in your comfort zone complaining about the unfairness of life than to use your influence to change things? I answered yes to these questions. Making the admission worth the effort means not self-judging but just accepting that human beings are complex and we do the best we can at the time to respond to our needs. It doesn't make us bad people, it just makes us human. But if we don't use what we've learned to move ourselves forward? Well, maybe that's when we should start beating ourselves up!

You already know everything you need to produce your best ever performance

Events happen, we interpret them to create an experience that we store in our subconscious. So why aren't we already effective? The reasons may be:

- The way we interpreted the event – which caused us to believe something that isn't realistic. Did we miss some of the lessons by only looking at it one way?

- We're only working with our conscious mind (our logic) – so we're not listening to our subconscious mind (our intuition). And if we're doing that, we aren't accessing all our experience in making our interpretation.

■ We're only working with our subconscious – operating on autopilot and not using our conscious mind to check that what we're doing is logical. And if we're doing that, we're acting like children in situations that require us to act like adults.

The only way to be effective is to have your logic and intuition in balance . . . it's only common sense, after all.

Using this book to trigger your subconscious knowledge and insight

If people learn from experience, what's the point of reading a book? No point at all, if you don't make it into an experience. Remember:

Event + interpretation = experience

So if you just read the book, you've had an event not an experience and you won't learn anything from it. A good book will do three things:

■ It will make you think, interpret and maybe challenge some of your beliefs and, in doing so, will become an 'experience' in its own right.

■ It will bring to the surface things you already know on a subconscious level from your experience of life so you can look more closely at them.

■ It will expose you to someone else's experience so you can learn from that in the same way that you learn from your own experience and, in doing so, save yourself time and aggravation.

But it won't work if you read it on autopilot

I hope that as you read the rest of the book, you will pause every time something I say triggers either of the following responses:

- If you want to say 'well, that's just common sense' – stop and ask yourself 'am I acting on what I know?' and 'would other people be able to tell that's what I believe from the way I behave?'

- If you get an 'off' feeling – stop and work out what's making you feel like that. You don't have to agree with everything I say. My insight is only here to trigger yours – it's what makes sense to you that matters.

IN SHORT

▶ **We do what makes sense to us so suspend self-judgement and look for your logic.** What do you have to gain when your influencing attempts go wrong?

▶ **If we're not as effective as we'd like to be, we need to reinterpret our experiences.** Looking back to your last experience of influencing, what might a neutral observer say you'd missed?

▶ **A good book will trigger things your subconscious knows already.** What has made sense to you so far?

PART

2

■ *real* management for the way it is ■

Getting influencing right in the *real* world

▶ **Being too process-orientated gets us into more trouble than we know**

If you're anything like me, you've skipped straight to this page because it explains the influencing process from first thoughts to final review for learning. Never mind telling me why it goes wrong, I hear you mutter, just tell me how to do it right. I wish I could but, sadly:

- Learning is about trial and error and the more you can learn from my trials and errors [in Part 1] the less time you need to waste doing your own.

- When it comes to getting results in the real world, you can't pin your faith on the kind of task-orientated processes that operate in most organizations. Why not? Because human beings have a habit of putting spanners in the works of even the best laid processes.

Process is important, I grant you [there's really no other way to get from start to finish in anything we do] but a process that's been designed without a proper understanding of what *can* go wrong, *will* go wrong.

How many times have you felt that you were serving a process that should be there to serve you? On my good days, I see process as a necessary evil and on my bad days it's the enemy that makes me manage like a robot. And speaking of enemies, I like the martial arts idea of deflecting your opponent's strength against itself, so I design inclusive processes that take account of all the things that normal processes leave out, things that make me more people-orientated.

▶ It's not my process that matters – it's yours

Most management writers will tell you 'follow this process and you'll be fine'. I only wish it were true. But the truth is, no one but you can know what it's like in your world, so no one but you can design an influencing process that works for you. What I can do is describe seven generic steps that will identify all the things you need to think about when you're designing your own influencing process. So, as you read through each step, remember the insights you got from reading Part 1 and think about how you can use the process to help you address those issues.

10

How do you ensure your influencing process will work?

Understanding the variables so you can manage the dynamic

Getting your head around the influencing variables

When people design processes, they start by getting their heads round the variables the process is being designed to manage. Once the process is designed, however, it tends to be followed automatically and with no further thought given to the variables.

When we're designing a new process we use original thinking but, because our brain doesn't like original thinking, as soon as we develop the process, it lays it down in our hard-wiring so

To avoid autopilot always think afresh about the available.

that whenever it is stimulated into thinking the process is needed, it can just bring it out and run it on autopilot. Running on autopilot can be helpful (you don't want to have to use original thinking every time you put your hand on something hot) but it can also be hindering – especially when dealing with people. To avoid any risk of my acting on autopilot, I design all my processes so the first step involves always thinking afresh about the variables.

Real influencing is about winning hearts and minds

In the subtitle to this book I describe influencing as 'winning hearts and minds to achieve goals'. I deliberately used an expression people can relate to rather than one which more accurately describes what influencing actually does. Well, 'how to convince people on a conscious and subconscious level to achieve goals' doesn't have quite the same ring to it, does it?

When someone is committed, doing the right thing is second nature.

When we've won people's 'hearts and minds' they have conviction, enthusiasm and a light in their eyes when they talk about the thing they're committed to. What makes people behave that way is when they believe something both on a conscious and subconscious level and when believing it creates positive experiences.

The acid test of a 'hearts and minds' commitment is when people walk their talk – and not just on the big stuff where they're making considered responses, but in the small stuff when they're acting on autopilot, responding from their subconscious (what we tend to call instinct). When someone is committed on this level, doing the right thing is second nature. And helping someone get to that point over a goal that is important to you – well, that's real influence. And that's what this book is about.

It's about changing what's in their heads

When we think about influencing someone, we tend to think about changing their behaviour. But action follows thought, and behaviour is only the visible expression of a belief so real influencing involves changing someone's belief. One of the

Real influencing involves changing someone's belief. most important lessons I've ever learned as a manager is that trying to change people's behaviour is a frustrating, energy-draining waste of time. You may think it's worked because you can get people to behave differently for a while, with constant monitoring and pressure. But you can't actually change someone else. Only they can. And only when they change what's in their heads. Let me give you some examples.

In my late teens and twenties, I tried a variety of alcoholic drinks but never found one I liked and I came to believe I'm not much of a drinker. It wasn't a matter of high moral principle – believe me it's no fun being the only sober person at the party – it was just a picky set of taste buds. Then, in my thirties, I went to Australia for six months and fell in love with the taste of Australian red wine. Now, you can buy some excellent Australian red wine in this country, and for a few months after my return, I got into the habit of going to the drinks aisle at the supermarket (a new behaviour for me) and buying some. But even though I liked the taste as much at home as I had in Oz, I eventually slipped back into my old shopping habits and stopped going to the drinks aisle. I may have changed my drinking behaviour for a while there, but I guess I never really changed my belief that I'm not much of a drinker.

If you're a smoker who's been trying to give up, you might relate to the words of wisdom in a book on giving up that said trying to change your habits doesn't work and you'll always be a smoker until you start thinking of yourself as a non-smoker. Of course, if real life were as simple as that, everyone who wanted to give up smoking would have done it by now just by thinking of themselves as a non-smoker. But though this advice is true as far as it goes, it oversimplifies the complexity of the real-life situation. Because no one belief ever stands on its own. It's part of a complex web of beliefs that become a frame of reference, a way of making sense of the world. So, the friend who'd bought the book didn't just believe she was a smoker, she believed that a meal wasn't over until she'd had a cigarette, she believed that she wasn't awake until she'd had her first cup of coffee and cigarette, she believed that if she gave up smoking, she'd get fat, she believed . . . well, you get the picture. Yes, our beliefs are at the root of all the things we do but it isn't as simple as it sounds.

Am I depressing you about the likely chances of your being able to influence anyone successfully? Well, if I am, don't worry because it's not nearly as hard as it sounds. It's just different to the methods we're used to using, like persuasion and argument. And influencing, like all real managing, is just a matter of understanding the complexity so you can find the simplicity.

To achieve goals

We need to influence people to achieve our goals and real influencing is the difference between someone signing up to our goals and thinking your goals are their goals. When you're thinking about the variables, you need to factor in the kind of goals you have in mind. Think about an issue on which you're currently trying to influence someone. What's your goal? Does it involve a big or small change on the part of the person you're trying to influence? Are the stakes high or low? Is it a stand-alone goal or does it connect with lots of other goals you're also trying to achieve? How big is the belief they'll need to challenge? Is it essential to your success in the job or only desirable? Is it a widespread issue (with lots of people who have to be influenced) or a contained issue (with only one or two)?

The influencer and influenced are variables too

Understanding yourself as an influencer and the people you're seeking to influence is so critical to the success of any influencing process that I've singled them out as steps in their own right and put them in the next chapter.

As is the culture of influencing in your organization

I once worked in a macho environment where intuition, instinct and gut feelings were disparaged so rational, logical argument was the cultural norm for influencing. How would you describe the influencing culture in your organization? Is it formal (reports, presentations) or informal (corridor lobbying)? Is it based on position power (your place in the hierarchy says how much influence you have) or expert power (the more knowledge and expertise you have the higher your influence)? Is it about what you know or who you know? Are employees who know the place inside out or consultants who bring an outsider's view listened to most by the powers that be? Are arguments that appeal to logic or instinct (head or heart) valued most? Obviously, I'm talking either/or here when really it's a continuum but you can usually tell which pole your organization is closer to. Not sure about your organization's influencing culture? Think about the most influential person you know and analyze what makes them influential and that will give you your answer.

Timescale is a variable too

How long do you have to achieve your results? In the example in Part 1, I was lucky. I was managing a big change with a long timescale so I had the time I needed to influence at belief level, although even then I knew the sooner I got my team on board the more time I'd have to achieve the culture change strategy. Your approach to influencing will need to reflect how much time you have but a word of warning. Don't artificially reduce the amount of time you have. If there is a genuine crisis looming, that'll help you speed things up because it'll help you generate dissatisfaction more easily but don't create an artificial crisis as people will suss you out. And remember, you want your influence to be self-sustaining so it's worth putting in the time now to save endless 'propping up' later.

Above all, it's a dynamic that changes over time

The complexity of the dynamic comes from the fact that each variable doesn't just affect the influencing process, it acts on the other variables too. And it changes over time because whether we are conscious of it or not, we're always influencing people and being influenced by them.

Influence is not to be confused with power

Let's be clear about this because most books on influencing that I've read over the years confuse the two. Not that I blame them. I mean, for goodness' sake, even the dictionary defines influence as the *power* to affect others so how confusing is that? Well, forgive me for arguing (although I'm sure it was just sloppy articulation on their part and they used power but meant *ability* to affect others) but, in the real world, influence and power are two completely different things. Influence requires

In the *real* world, influence and power are two completely different things.

equality between people and an adult/adult relationship. Power requires inequality and the kind of parent/child relationship that is inherent in the concept of hierarchy.

It's hard to be genuinely influential with people over whom you have power and authority. Yet, ironically, influence is more powerful than power (and yes, I can see now why the dictionary people had problems with their definition). That's because power is an external force acting on a person whereas influence is an internal force, acting on a person from inside their own head.

It's hard but it's not impossible to be genuinely influential with your team. You can do it by never pulling rank, by treating your team in the same way as you'd treat a colleague. I'm not talking about a democracy (I believe in managers managing), I'm talking about a management style that is built on managing-by-influence not managing-by-exerting-authority.

Or with manipulation

I've given this issue a chapter in its own right too as you need to think about it afresh every time you set out to influence someone. The dictionary is even more confusing about manipulating than it is about influencing. It defines it as 'to manage artfully, often in an unfair way' – which leaves me wanting to:

- Look up the definition of 'artfully' to see whether it's good or bad (the dictionary says it's good but the first connotation that came into my head was the 'artful dodger').

- Ask why they said 'often' unfair rather than 'always' which implies they think there are occasions when manipulating someone else is fair.

I say influencing is fair and manipulation is unfair. There's a lot more on this in Chapter 12 but for now, let's just remember that.

IN SHORT

▶ **Managing the influencing process is about managing the variables.** How do the people and organizational variables affect your influencing process?

▶ **Influence is about changing what's in people's heads.** What's your best experience of changing the way someone thinks and how did you do it?

▶ **It's hard to be genuinely influential with people you manage.** If I asked your team, would they say they listened to you because you're influential or because you're the boss?

11

How do you avoid the 'persuasion' trap and build your process round the 'people element'?

Understanding yourself as an influencer and the people you're seeking to influence

The 'persuasion' trap

This is a double whammy. First, when people persuade by marshalling their best arguments they focus on what makes sense to them . . . yet everyone's logic is different. Second, as an externally imposed approach, it only appeals to the conscious mind . . . but it's the subconscious where people store their beliefs. In short, it doesn't work. Sometimes it looks like it's worked but it doesn't last.

Not that we're in either/or territory

My 'both/and' philosophy can look like fence-sitting. But I do believe things aren't inherently bad or good, only helpful or hindering depending on the context and the experience we create from them. So, though I'd like you to avoid falling into the trap of relying on persuasion, persuasion can have a role to play in the influencing process. It's just it works best as part of a more rounded approach. And it goes without saying that it only works when it's based on their logic not yours.

What kind of influencer are you?

It's not the message that influences it's the messenger, so knowing yourself as an influencer is essential. What's your best ever experience of influencing? How did you do it? What skills and characteristics did you use? Why was it so successful? What can you learn about yourself and your style of influencing from that experience? What was your worst ever experience of influencing? What has that experience taught you? In general, what characteristic (knowledge, belief, attitude, behaviour, skill) do you most rely on when you're influencing? And in what circumstances does that characteristic work against you?

Consider what your answers have shown you. Do you see your relationships with people as an end in their own right or as a means of achieving your goals? Think about whether you're a proactive influencer or a reactive one. Whether you prefer to appeal to logic or emotions. Whether you prefer direct influence (putting a different point of view) or indirect influence (asking questions to challenge their opinion). Do you rely too much on charm and charisma? Or on conviction and enthusiasm? And does your approach work better with some people than others?

Who pushes your buttons?

Another way of finding out what kind of influencer you are is to look at the kind of people who push your buttons when they're trying to influence you. Let me give you an example. I was in a meeting with a colleague (not well known for her tact and diplomacy) and an external consultant. The consultant was trying to sell us her services and she was using what I call the 'boundless enthusiasm' approach. I don't know if it was the relentlessly upbeat tone, the synchronized gesticulation or the dogmatic certainty that this was the only way to go that scared me most but I was exhausted by the end of it and it was only by an act of supreme self-control that I didn't do her actual bodily harm (only to pin her arms to her sides to stop her taking off, you understand). After she'd gone, I was about to say how irritating I'd found her when my colleague said I must have really enjoyed her presentation as she was so like me! I was horrified. I went back to my team, told them my sorry tale and, instead of the sympathy I deserved, they just said 'well, duh'. Oh dear. The technical term for this is projecting.

We're **projecting** when we see in others something that we have in ourselves but don't see. It can be a thought, a belief, a characteristic, anything. There is usually something in the other person that gives us a hook to hang our projection on but our projection is coming from us and not from them.

Okay, your turn. What do the people who push your buttons tell you about yourself? And if you're in denial about the answers, ask someone you trust for feedback . . . because denial is part of projection.

What about the people you need to influence

For anything you're trying to achieve, there are two groups of stakeholders involved.

> I divide **stakeholders** into **interest** and **impact groups**. Impact groups can prevent you achieving the outcomes. Interest groups will be affected by the outcome but can't prevent you achieving the outcomes. You can't ignore the needs of either group, but the distinction helps when you're managing a conflict of interests.

It's essential to influence the impact groups and desirable to influence the interest groups. But, for the people in each of these groups, do you know what matters most to them, what motivates them, what beliefs they hold that govern their behaviour and the way they make sense of their world? I'm not just talking about the specific issue on which you're influencing, I'm talking about seeing them as real people who have a lot more going on than just your stuff.

Pick someone you're trying to influence at the moment and analyze them. Think of something they've done recently – an effect they've created, a result they've achieved – one they're happy with. Now, ask yourself 'what would someone have to believe (about themselves, other people, the world at large) to see that as a positive result?' Then think about the things they did to achieve the result and ask, 'what would someone have to believe to think that behaviour would produce that result?' Now try the same analysis again but this time with an effect they're not happy with.

See people as *real* people who have a lot more going on than just your stuff.

Listening on two levels

Another way of understanding the people you want to influence is to listen on two levels to the things they say – to find out what they're implying by what they say, what they're leaving unsaid and what they're telling you indirectly. It can be lots of fun (oh dear, how sad do I sound?). Let me give you an example I heard on TV the other day. An opposition politician was complaining to an interviewer about the Prime Minister. He'd asked the Prime Minister what he'd do if he failed to get international agreement on an important issue. The Prime Minister said he wasn't going to answer hypothetical questions. The opposition politician accused the Prime Minister of refusing to be straight with the British people. With almost comic timing, the interviewer asked the opposition politician whether he would put political differences aside and support the Prime Minister if he did decide to take unilateral action. The opposition politician replied that he didn't answer hypothetical questions. Well, it made *me* laugh. And before you accuse me of being political, let me tell you that when I listen on two levels I hear this kind of thing across all political parties and in all walks of life, so I'm being illustrative not partisan. It's only human nature for *my* refusal to answer hypothetical questions to be *your* deceitful avoidance tactics. Honest!

Still, in case I didn't influence you with that example, here's one you can try at work. Next time you hear someone start a sentence with 'with all due respect' listen on two levels and see if what they're saying is actually respectful. I'll bet you here and now it's not. Or try listening on two levels for people who start sentences with 'I don't mean to be rude' or 'in all fairness' or – well, you get my drift, yes?

Just don't assume you're right

You'll learn a lot about the people you're seeking to influence just by reviewing what you already know about them. But remember – you're guessing so you'll need to find ways of checking your understanding.

IN SHORT

▶ **The kind of influencer you are will affect the way you influence.** How would a trusted colleague describe your influencing style?

▶ **The same approach won't work with everyone.** Do you vary your approach for different people?

▶ **The things people say tell you so much more than the words suggest.** How often do you listen on two levels?

12

How do you get clarity about what you want?

Setting your intentions and principles so you influence with integrity

Aligning your conscious and subconscious intentions

In my experience, lack of clarity of intention is the most common reason why influencing fails. It sounds hard to believe because if you ask anyone who is trying to influence, they always sound clear about their intention. In influencing, as in life, our goals are a product of our conscious mind but our intentions can be products of either our conscious or subconscious minds. When our conscious and subconscious minds have conflicting intentions, our subconscious mind, being stronger, will materialize its intentions at the expense of our conscious ones. So, if at a conscious level my intention is to influence someone to change their behaviour but at a subconscious level I actually gain benefits from the behaviour I'm trying to change, I may well fail to be influential. That sounds like psychobabble (probably because it is – it's the theory underpinning the concept of co-dependency) so let me give you a real-life story.

My goal (my conscious intention) with my team members was to create empowered, independent people who can solve problems and make good quality decisions without constantly referring to me. So, how come I often end up creating the exact opposite? Well, when I ask myself what I have to gain from creating dependants, I find I get a big buzz out of being needed. Hey presto, dependent team members!

If you want to avoid this risk, before you go anywhere near the person or people you want to influence, first put your conscious intentions to the acid test by asking yourself what you might gain if your influencing failed. Listen hard to your answer and be honest with yourself. If you have a lot to gain from failing, dig deeper to expose the fears and beliefs that underlie your conflicting intentions. Then choose.

- You can accept that your subconscious knows best and adjust your conscious intention so that you are influencing to a different goal.

- If you think your beliefs are hindering (and you'll know this because if they are they'll have produced negative experiences) challenge them and replace them with helpful beliefs, which allows your subconscious to adjust its intention to align with your conscious intention.

The added benefit of congruence

Congruence – that happy state where our conscious and subconscious intentions are aligned and creating positive experiences – isn't just important because it stops you self-sabotaging the influencing process. It's also the state you need to be in for real influencing because it's what makes people believe in you.

Have a hierarchy of objectives

Next, you need to consider the context within which you are pursuing your intention as no intention stands in isolation. This means thinking about what else you want to achieve during your influencing process. Have you ever experienced someone who focuses single-mindedly on one thing only to find that in the end they've lost everything else? Well, that applies in influencing as much as in life. My background is in Human Resource Management and I've seen many a manager sacrifice their relationship with the unions for the sake of winning a specific issue and I've seen others who gave up on an issue that was critical to the future of the organization to preserve their relationship with the unions. There will always be more than one objective in any influencing process even if it's only as basic as getting your proposals agreed *and* having good relationships with the people you are influencing. Putting your objectives in order of importance will help you later if you need to make choices.

Put 'honouring your principles' at the top

The funny thing about principles is we often don't even realize they're there until we're under pressure to sacrifice them. So, think now about what you won't do to win people over. About what would make you feel bad about yourself if you gave it up for the sake of winning people over. These are your principles. A quick word of caution about principles – the word being 'dogmatic'. Principles are just strongly held beliefs that guide our decisions and behaviour and beliefs are just thoughts we haven't questioned in a long time. Being willing to question is the difference between being principled and being dogmatic. So, before you commit to honouring your principles above all else, make sure you've taken a long, hard look at them.

Speaking of principles – the fine line between influencing and manipulating

This is also the stage in the influencing process when you must factor in the checks and balances that will ensure you don't inadvertently become manipulative. Things like:

- *Not being selective in your information giving* – give people the downside of your proposals so they're not basing their decision on a distorted picture.

- *Not deciding on their behalf what's best for someone else* – beware the whole parent/child 'I know what's best for you' trap by treating people like adults.

- *Not asking people to commit to something you know is not in their interests* – just because it's in yours. Be ruthless in your self-examination.

- *Engaging with people as real people* – don't be tempted to see them as one dimensional influencing targets or pawns in a game.

- *Being clear about what you want or need* – even if there are great benefits for the other person, you should still say what's in it for you.

- *Being open about your methods* – asking questions that get people to look at something a different way is the simplest and most powerful way to change what's in people's heads. But it's indirect and risks being manipulative. But not if you tell people, 'I'm just trying to get you to look at it a different way to see if it changes your position.'

But this is my list and you're not me so it's your list that counts. Think back to times when you've felt manipulated and work out what it was the other person did (or didn't do) that made you feel that way? Then, if it's not on my list, put it on yours.

Managing the influencing paradox – conviction with flexibility

One final thought. I don't know anyone who is influenced by people who don't speak with conviction about their issue. I mean, if they can't convince themselves, right? And yet, paradoxically, we aren't influenced by people who are so convinced they're right, they're not open to being influenced themselves. Have you ever tried to sound convinced and open at the same time? Well, I've got one more thinking task for you before you go and see the people you're seeking to influence.

Look at your objectives and your principles and decide what is a conviction point and what is flexible. Only you can do this for your issue but I work with the following 'rule' – everything, except my principles, is flexible. I speak with conviction about my principles and how my proposals achieve those principles but I try to stay open to other ways of achieving those principles.

IN SHORT

▶ **Congruence is the key to effective influencing.** Do you sometimes achieve intentions you didn't know you had?

▶ **We all have principles, we just aren't always aware of them.** How clear are you about the principles that guide your day-to-day decisions?

▶ **Know the difference between influencing and manipulating.** Have you ever crossed the line?

13

How do you get clarity about what they want?

Engaging with *real* people and their issues

Now, put everything you've done so far to one side

I know, I know. What on earth am I playing at? If I didn't want you to use what we've done so far, why didn't I just put this step first? Two reasons:

- When we talk to other people, we interpret what they say before we react to it. And interpreting means running it past our frame of reference. This happens at a subconscious level so we can't be sure what's in the frame of reference unless we've just had it out and looked at it.

- We're all subconsciously influenced by what other people say to us and, if we talk to them before we have clarity in our own minds, we risk being influenced in ways we may later regret.

I accept I'm pushing my luck telling you not to think about it because our hard-wiring makes it impossible. When I tell you not to think of a pink elephant – what happens? Exactly. If you want to stop thinking about one thing you have to think about another. So, asking you to think about a purple horse would do the trick much better. That's the technique you need to use here. Don't try to force yourself not to think of your own issues, just focus on them and let that do it for you.

Rapport is out, relate is in

There are lots of books out there with all sorts of techniques for building rapport. There are people in the NLP (neuro-linguistic programming) movement making a fortune from teaching you how to artificially mirror people so they'll think you're like them. Well, my advice is don't bother doing the rapport thing. Because no matter how good you get at the technique, people can always tell even if only on a subconscious level.

When we're observing and listening, our conscious picks up the words and the more obvious behaviour and our subconscious picks up the rest. Because **our subconscious notices everything** and because it's stronger than our conscious, we tend to form our judgements from the way people behave *not* from what they say. Our **subconscious is designed to spot inconsistencies,** which it tells us about through our intuition. Because all this happens below our level of consciousness, we often just get a feeling that we don't trust someone, but if we analyzed it, we'd find we've picked up an inconsistency between their words and deeds.

I suggest you do the 'relate' thing instead. You know the difference, right? Okay you may not have thought about it consciously so you may not be able to define it off the bat, but you know it on an experiential level. When you're relating to someone, each understands where the other is coming from even if you're not coming from the same place and it feels okay, two-way, real and completely different from when you know you're being buttered up for a reason by someone trying to build rapport with you. In a relationship built on rapport it always feels just a little too good to be true, slightly surreal and almost certainly one-way.

The 'visiting princess' effect

I worked with someone who is brilliant at building rapport but hopeless at relating. When you first talk to him, he gives you his complete attention, asks you a lot of questions and seems genuinely interested in your answers. You feel like you really matter but when you take the same interest in return he's evasive, giving nothing away. I call it the 'visiting princess' effect because the old cynic in you knows that the attention a princess pays you isn't real, and that though you'll remember how good it felt to matter, once she's moved on to the next person she'll be doing the same with them and will have forgotten all about you. You felt it but she didn't. She was just doing her job. Which is fair enough when you're a visiting princess – after all, no one is trying to claim her visit is anything more than an opportunity for you to bask in the warmth of her undivided attention for a few moments – but it's not okay to do it in real life. In *real* life, you owe it to people to be *real* with them.

In *real* life, you owe it to people to be *real* with them.

Relating to the people you're seeking to influence

I'm distinguishing between 'rapport' and 'relate' because rapport is manipulative and relating is influential. Relating to people means:

- *Looking for what is unique about each person* – so that you don't see them as targets but as real people.

- *Making an effort to understand them* – and staying open-minded about them until you've worked out where they're coming from.

- *Finding an honest level on which you can relate to them* – no two people come from exactly the same place but if you keep looking you *will* find something you can build on.

Learning about people from your conversations with them

The best way to learn about people is to listen to their stories. Our stories tell people so much more about us than the simple events we're describing. Listen to the language people use and the interpretations they put on events to create their experience. Listen to what they imply and what they leave out and you will learn about their beliefs and their intentions (both conscious and subconscious).

You already do this all the time. Don't believe me? Think about someone you know who has a big problem that they've told you all about. Now, tell me – from the way they talked about their problem – what did you learn about their attitudes to problems? Do they see them as challenges to rise to, as an inevitable fact of life or do they see themselves as one of life's unfortunate victims? Now think of someone else you know who has a problem but who has a completely different attitude to it. How do you know their attitude is different? What are you picking up from their story that makes you know that? See. I told you. You can do this stuff already – it's just that you do it on a subconscious level and that exercise was about bringing it up into your conscious.

A good way of getting people to tell you the stories that will help you learn about their views on your issue is to ask them what the most frustrating aspect of it is for them. So, if you're trying to influence a team member to improve their customer focus, ask what the most frustrating thing about dealing with customers is. Influencing is about changing what's in people's heads and, to do that, you have to find out what's in there already. And in asking about the frustrations in their current situation you do two other important things:

- You start the process of gently stimulating their dissatisfaction with the current state which is a prerequisite for change.

- You can find the hook that gets them to listen later on when you're ready to do your influencing.

If you can, help them get their own clarity

As I said, you can guess at people's beliefs and intentions from the stories they tell you, but often they aren't that aware of them, themselves. That's because, unlike you – who's been through the earlier steps and got your own clarity – they'll still have a lot of their beliefs, principles and intentions buried at a subconscious level. You can use the questions I asked you before to help them get their own clarity.

Also, try listening to articulate. Do this by listening to what they're saying and feeding it back to them. Not like a touchy-

Listening to articulate can change what's in people's heads in its own right. feely counsellor responding to an 'I'm unhappy' with a 'you're unhappy'. I mean feeding back what you got from listening on two levels to their stories and checking your understanding with them. I call it listening to articulate because often when people are talking about deeply held beliefs, they aren't as articulate as they normally are. So you're articulating it for them. It's about translating from fuzzy to clear so it makes more sense to them than it did when they said it (or implied it). Listening to articulate is a technique that can change what's in people's heads in its own right by surfacing something at a conscious level that was there in their subconscious, influencing their reactions and behaviour in a way that, now they're conscious of it, they don't want it to do.

Don't try to influence them at this stage

However, the aim of this step is not influencing but helping people get to the same level of clarity about their issues as you are about yours and to enable you to understand what their issues are. Of course, having said we influence people all the time by who we are, I'm not saying you won't be having an influence on some level during this step. I'm just saying don't try to influence them on the specific subject. Be real with them and let who you are influence them. Trust in the fact that all the effort you put into getting your own clarity and congruence at the earlier stages will pay off for you now. Understand that being yourself will be what gives you the foundation from which to build the two-way influencing relationship you need if you're going to win hearts and minds.

But do give back if they look for it

Having made a big fuss about people who do one-way traffic (when talking about rapport versus relating) I want to be absolutely clear about this next point. For the sake of describing influencing as a process (which is a convenient framework but nevertheless an artificial way of describing something that is in effect a way of being rather than an act of doing) I'm separating the get-off-to-a-good-start-entry-level step from the two-way-influencing-relationship-building step which I describe in the next chapter. But in real life, these two steps don't always separate out that neatly, you move backwards and forwards between them as the relationship develops. For example, you might well be at the two-way influencing stage of a work relationship with a colleague but when you join the same departmental ten pin bowling team, you're back at entry level in the social part of your relationship.

What I'm saying is, in general, focus on them and on understanding their issues, needs and wants and leave talking about your own until the next step. But don't deliberately withhold your own views if they ask you about them because that way leads to rapport not relating and it may leave them not wanting to move to the next step. So, keep an eye on how things are developing and be flexible in your approach. Some people will be very open about their own issues and just not be that terribly interested in yours so this step will seem like a separate step in the process. But other people will be as interested in you as you are in them so the edges of this step and the next one will become blurry. It's not a problem so long as you remember and apply the advice in the next chapter as soon as you feel you've started reaching the two-way point.

Not just another step in the process – an ongoing activity

While I'm talking about the flaws in the notion of an influencing 'process' let me make one more point. The thing I don't like about processes is that they always come across like you're supposed to do each step in sequence when in real life it's never that easy. And that's particularly true of this step which isn't a discrete step that you do once then move on. The kind of conversations I'm describing here should be going on all the time because being a good manager isn't just about being able to influence certain people on certain issues at certain times. It's about being influential all the time. So take whatever opportunities you get to understand the people around you.

IN SHORT

 Build relationships not rapport. How real are you with the people you are seeking to influence?

 Focus on them but don't hold back if asked. When you're influencing, do you talk more than you listen?

 Don't try to influence before you've put foundations in place. Have you ever been tempted to just leap in with a hard sell?

14

How do you build a two-way influencing relationship?

Putting foundations in place before you raise the issue

Calling on all your relationship skills

In this chapter, which is designed to cover the ground between relating and raising the issue, I'm going to assume prior general knowledge because building relationships is a book in its own right, maybe even a number of volumes in an encyclopaedic series and I only have one chapter! But just to summarize lessons we've all learned from the university of life – a successful relationship takes, among other things, time, attention, regularity of contact, common interests, space, communication, understanding, mutual disclosure of information (at a mutually acceptable pace) and a sense of connection on one or more of the four levels (mental, emotional, spiritual and physical) depending on what kind of relationship it is.

What follows are a few important points relating specifically to the 'influencing' part of the two-way influencing relationship concept, highlighting issues where an influencing relationship perhaps varies from the norm.

The tricky concept of mutual disclosure

A relationship starts with the sharing of information. The experts use the expression mutual disclosure to describe the way we swap information with each other at increasing levels of intimacy (the research suggests we start with facts, move on to feelings and then to values). In other words, I tell you where I live and you reciprocate by telling me where you live, then I tell you I don't enjoy living in my current area and you tell me how you feel about living in your place and so it goes. It's one of those things that you don't really notice when it is happening in sync but you do notice when it's not.

For example, I have two friends: one shares things the other person really doesn't want to know and wouldn't disclose about themselves and who, when such disclosures seem imminent holds up her hand, laughs and says TMI (too much information). They manage their differences well, but relationships work best when disclosure levels are pretty even and when progressive disclosure of increasingly personal information happens at a similar rate for each person.

In a two-way influencing relationship you need to remember that in the previous step you focused on their disclosure and although you didn't hold back when asked, you tried to keep your focus on them and not dominate the conversation with your own stuff. So, remember the mutual disclosure concept and make sure you get on level terms with them during this stage of the process.

Telling your stories

The best way to get on level terms with them is not to talk directly about your beliefs and principles – and not just because it always sounds artificial even when it's real – but to tell your own stories and let them work you out. Just as you encouraged the other person to do at the last stage, talking about what frustrates you about the current situation and why gives them a chance to work you out for themselves and they'll have more faith in that.

Finding your common purpose

We form relationships to meet needs and when they succeed it's because we found a common purpose (whether it was articulated or not). Sometimes, sadly, it only becomes obvious what the common purpose was, when one of the parties has changed direction and the common purpose no longer exists. The Human Resources function talks about the psychological contract (to distinguish it from the employment contract) which is the unspoken exchange between an organization and its employees. I know an organization in which a relaxed atmosphere, job security, and plenty of time for corridor socializing was an important part of the psychological contract and made up for the relatively low salaries so when the senior managers launched an efficiency drive people started to feel short-changed. Ironically enough, because they'd never articulated the psychological contract, they focused all their discontent on the low salaries issue – which had never been the issue before and wasn't the issue now but somehow became the vehicle for expressing their dissatisfaction.

A common purpose doesn't have to be some grand vision or complex set of interconnected objectives. Successful friendships have been built around a single shared interest. But if, in a two-way influencing relationship, the common purpose is bigger than the issue of substance and articulated, agreed and understood by both parties it will act as a self-regulator later on when the issue is raised.

Two-way means two-way

Yes, I know I'm stating the blindingly obvious here but you know, if it were that obvious, there'd be a lot fewer people who think influence is about getting people to do what you want. If you want to be influential, you must be open to being influenced yourself. You can't just listen to what people are saying; you must really *hear* it.

Think about how you respond to questions

How do you know if you're in a two-way influencing relationship or just a target for someone's persuasion? Ask a question and see what happens. If you're a target, the persuader will have a ready answer to the question, seeing your question purely as a chance to do more persuading. If they see you as a real person, they'll stop and think about the question and be just as likely to respond with a question of their own because they're engaging with you and the issues that prompted your question. In other words, your question will have influenced their thinking. How do you respond to questions from people you're trying to influence?

IN SHORT

▶ **An influencing relationship is as complex as any other relationship.** Do you see your influencing relationships as being somewhat one-dimensional?

▶ **Influencing is not about getting your own way.** Would a neutral observer accuse you of using your influencing skills just to get your own way?

▶ **The way you handle questions says a lot about the kind of influencer you are.** What is your reaction to questions from people you're seeking to influence?

15

How do you change what's in people's heads?

Understanding the mind's complexity and the two keys to *real* influencing

We're finally ready to raise the issue

By now, you may be wondering what kind of a crazy influencing process doesn't allow you to raise the actual issue until step six of a seven-step process. Well, what you've been doing so far is laying the important foundations – thinking, relating, establishing your credibility – so you are already influential in a general way with the person or people you're seeking to influence before you raise the specific issue.

But you don't always have the luxury of time

For something important you should bite the bullet and make time but this is the real world so here's another way of looking at the influencing process in this book. If you make the previous steps and the next step an integral part of your general management style then you can use this step on its own as your influencing process whenever you have a specific issue.

And if you have to go in cold with someone new, the two techniques described in this chapter are powerful enough to work on their own, but you should always go back afterwards and work through the process to build a two-way influencing relationship. I say this because both the techniques I describe in this chapter have the potential to be manipulative and the risk of that happening is higher when you're using them without a two-way influencing relationship to ground you.

The two techniques are simple but only if you have some understanding of the complexity of the way our minds work. So here we go.

The suggestibility of the subconscious mind

Have you seen Derren Brown's Mind Control programmes with their bizarre but fascinating experiments where people respond like they're hypnotized even though they're not and where it looks like he can read people's minds (which he's never claimed to be doing)? His experiments work with, among other things, the suggestibility of the human subconscious. And we're at our most suggestible when we're in what experts call 'an altered state of awareness'.

Perhaps the most well-known altered state of awareness is hypnosis. When we're hypnotized, our suggestible subconscious mind is not being held in check by our conscious mind, and the hypnotist can speak directly to it, planting ideas that our conscious mind might reject if it could hear them. But you don't have to be hypnotized to be in an altered state of awareness. Have you ever found yourself gazing out of the window at work daydreaming about something and coming to with a jolt

We're at our most suggestible when we're in 'an altered state of awareness'.

when someone speaks to you? Have you ever been in the flow, in the zone, so engaged with what you're doing that you didn't

Our subconscious mind is hard-wired not to let us do anything that will harm us.

notice time passing and didn't hear what was going on around you? Have you ever been listening to someone ramble on and on so you end up only half listening and, before you know it, you're nodding off?

In all these situations, we're in the altered state of awareness that puts our subconscious mind in charge . . . with two powerful consequences. The first is that we're very suggestible because our conscious mind, which stops us doing daft things, has been overpowered by our subconscious. The second is that we're very creative because in addition to being well known for its suggestibility, the subconscious is also well known for it's creativity – its power is released when we're in the zone.

Now, if you're a bit of a devil, tempted to see if you can use this information to get people to agree to things they wouldn't agree to normally, now might be a good time to tell you about two clever little failsafe mechanisms. One is that our subconscious mind is hard-wired not to let us do anything that will harm us. Two is that (even if the change isn't actually harmful), our minds won't sustain it if there isn't an alignment of conscious and subconscious intentions so, it's not enough to convince people on a subconscious level to influence them, you have to do it on a conscious level as well. OK, enough with the health warning, back to the complexity.

Speaking direct to people's subconscious

How can we access someone's subconscious, bearing in mind it's not morally acceptable to hypnotize your colleagues or good for your image to bore them to sleep? I've seen Derren

Brown speak directly to people's subconscious by talking non-stop in a warm comforting voice saying things that don't need answers. And when people realize that a response isn't necessary, they relax and disengage their conscious minds (which is what happens when we nod off in presentations). I've seen Paul McKenna speak directly to people's subconscious when he's helping them with phobias (as opposed to when he's hypnotizing people) by talking in an instructional tone of voice, again without seeking a response and so fast they don't have time to engage with what he's saying on a conscious level. When the amount of input coming at us is more than our conscious mind can handle, our subconscious mind takes up the slack.

Now, I'm not suggesting you need to become the next Derren Brown or Paul McKenna to be able to influence people. I'm only telling you this so you have a really clear idea of how powerful the results can be when you speak directly to someone's subconscious.

The subconscious reads non-verbal signals

The truth is, we already speak directly to people's subconscious all the time. We're just speaking from our subconscious so we're not aware of what we're 'saying'. And we don't just do it with words – we do it with our body, our tone of voice, our attitude. We've all come across the hype about there being a body language we can all learn to help us read people. Well, as is often the case with fashionable issues, people are taking a complex truth and, in their attempt to simplify and quantify it for you, they dumb it down to a ridiculous level. I mean does anyone actually believe that when 100 totally different people cross their arms you can interpret the gesture the same way for each one. Body language exists but it's a lot more complex than the books and courses would have us believe.

But, not to worry, because we don't need lessons. We're already unconsciously competent at reading body language because our subconscious is picking it up all the time. Okay, we don't always get it right (because life's like that) but then we don't always get it right when we're interpreting what people say in verbal language. We learn body language like we learn everything else – by the trial and error of our experience.

And it reads between the lines of what people say too

Our subconscious is designed to fill in all the gaps left by our conscious mind. It's this ability that I'm trying to bring to a conscious level in the 'listening on two levels' and 'listening to articulate' techniques. So, in addition to reading the non-verbal signals, our subconscious does a simultaneous translation of the words we're actually hearing when someone speaks to us. That translation includes what they're implying covertly by what they're saying overtly, what they're leaving unsaid and so on. Our subconscious is so clever, it can weave a rich tapestry of interpretative information from a single sentence. I've even made a dinner party game out of it where someone makes a statement and the rest of us deduce further information from it and the speaker tells us if we're right or not. Go on, try it and see. If I told you that the most frightening thing that has ever happened to me was 'driving back to Brixton from the cinema one Sunday afternoon and finding ourselves in the middle of a riot, stuck behind a police van which was being pelted with stones' what else am I telling you?

Our subconscious can weave a rich tapestry of interpretative information from a single sentence.

Communicating from subconscious to subconscious

Of course, what the subconscious can do is much more complex and fascinating than just reading each other's non-verbal signals and filling in the gaps. It can have whole subconscious 'conversations' with people which go on at the same time or in lieu of conscious conversations. And no, I don't just mean those long-married couples who know without words when their partner is ready to leave the party.

Let's say there's someone approaching you. You're talking to a colleague so you only see them with half an eye in terms of what your conscious mind notices. But something in what they're wearing or the way they're walking gives off signals of aggression to your subconscious which is ever on the alert to keep you safe. While your conscious mind isn't even aware that you've thought it, your subconscious will have picked up the signals, processed them, come to a conclusion *and* generated an autopilot response based on its experience of similar stimuli. And yes, there *will* be a response. Because even if, on a conscious level, you're maintaining an air of professional neutrality, your subconscious will be doing something. Maybe it will be making you tense up very slightly, maybe making you smile at them without making eye contact. But whatever it is you're doing, you can bet the subconscious of the person approaching you will be picking it up and reacting. And so the subconscious conversation goes on. You might be having a perfectly civilized conversation on the surface but there's a pretty tense conversation going on at subconscious level.

By the way, this is an example of what's happening when we get an 'off' feeling about someone, a feeling that there's something not quite right, that we don't trust them. We're having a different conversation at subconscious level to the one we're having at a conscious level so we get a sense that things are not what they seem even if we can't put our finger on exactly what's wrong.

Taking in information on two levels

What I'm saying is that our subconscious mind sees everything within our field of vision, but our conscious mind only sees what's important to us, what we need to process, because our minds would implode if our conscious minds had to process everything we see. Have you seen subliminal advertising – where a picture flashes up so quickly your conscious mind doesn't see it but it registers in your subconscious? That's an example of what I'm describing. And it's doesn't just happen with visual information. The same goes for information we take in through our other senses. We've all had experience of filtering out sounds that aren't important to us.

Our subconscious mind sees everything within our field of vision, but our conscious mind only sees what's important to us.

And becoming aware of times when our readings clash

There's an interesting consequence of our capacity to take in information on two levels. Let me tell you a story. There was a woman senior manager in an organization I used to work for and she intimidated everyone. She had a lot of power and she wasn't afraid to use it. It's no exaggeration to say people actually hated her. After my first few frustrating meetings with her I could see where they were coming from and I was tempted to go with the majority view but something about her didn't quite add up.

My intuition (which is the way our subconscious tries to communicate with us) was telling me that her terrorizing image was just that – an image, not the reality and that somewhere underneath was a vulnerable streak. As I said, she was a very powerful figure and it was important to the success of my culture change strategy that people started working more effectively with her, and vice versa. But I knew I wouldn't be able to influence anyone's view without something more than a gut feeling to back up my interpretation . . . so I started observing her.

I had help. The fact that the problem was on my conscious mind meant that my RAS started making sure my conscious noticed things that previously only my subconscious had noticed and, sure enough, one day it came to me. I was standing my ground with her about an issue – something people very rarely did – and I noticed her neck go red and blotchy. I'd never noticed it before but after that meeting I started noticing it all the time when she was confronting people. I realized that my subconscious had concluded from this signal that the real person was more nervous than her aggressive, this-is-not-negotiable style would suggest.

I know I can sound horribly moral-high-ground-ish when I bang on about not judging people but it's not for moral reasons that I say it, it's for practical reasons. Because once we make our minds up about someone, our RAS makes sure we don't see anything that would make us doubt our judgement. The people who hated this woman literally didn't see her red blotchy neck.

Creating subconscious expectations

Subconscious expectations are pre-programmes that tell us what to expect in certain situations or with certain people.

As we get to know people, our subconscious builds up a file of information on them based on our experience of them and it starts to expect certain reactions to certain stimuli. As it all happens on a subconscious level, we're not usually aware of our expectations until they react in a way that doesn't fit with them. You've had that experience, right? Typically, we feel they're acting out of character.

The senior manager in my story didn't have enough confidence to argue her case with people so she coped by giving off signals that created a subconscious expectation in others that it wasn't worth arguing with her. So, as if our subconscious isn't doing enough with its perception faculties and its ability to hold parallel conversations, it's also able to drive us to behave in ways that protect us from the things we fear or to meet needs that we didn't even know we had.

Thinking is the process of asking and answering questions

There's a lot more to our subconscious than I've had space to write about in this chapter but I've been neglecting the conscious mind so I need to move on to that before we get onto the techniques.

Have you ever listened to yourself think? Thinking involves asking ourselves questions and answering them and the quality of our thinking depends less on our so-called IQ level than on the quality of the question we ask ourselves. That's because the questions we ask shape the answers we get and, in doing that, they shape the direction of our thinking and often our emotions as well.

> I want to distinguish **emotions** from **feelings**. Emotions are mental states [coming from our thoughts] and feelings are physical sensations. Emotions can generate feelings as with anger and a tight feeling in the chest but they are separate. The same feeling can be associated with two emotions – for example, a churning stomach can be fear or excitement depending on our thoughts about the situation we're in.

Let me give you an example. You're running late for work, you turn on the tap in the kitchen to rinse a cup and it comes off in your hand, there's water everywhere. Your first thought is 'why does it always happen to me?' and you start remembering all the other bad things that have happened. Meanwhile you're now soaked and the kitchen is flooded. OK, let's rewind. The tap comes off in your hand, there's water everywhere. You think 'where's the stopcock?' – need I go on?

I developed a whole style of managing-by-asking-questions so I'm in danger of getting carried away. I'll contain my enthusiasm and just say that the right question can be an incredibly powerful way to shift someone's thinking. The habitual questions we ask ourselves shape the way we think of ourselves. I know someone who's always asking herself why she attracts men who treat her badly. Her repeated asking helps shape her image of herself as a hapless victim. I sometimes wish I had the nerve to ask her why she lets men treat her badly because I think if she asked that question she might end up changing her taste in men.

Influencing on two levels

I hope what I've said so far in this chapter has given you enough insight into the way our minds work for you to be able to see the importance of ensuring that your influencing works on both a conscious and subconscious level. And I hope I've given enough for you to get a grasp of the complexity to be able to appreciate the simplicity of the two techniques with which I'll close out this chapter.

Technique 1 – creating subconscious expectations

Somerset Maugham said 'It's a funny thing about life, if you refuse to accept anything but the best, you very often get it' and that's the thinking behind this technique. It's essentially just about projecting the response you want to get back and about responding to the other person in a way that encourages them to give you what you want – rewarding the helpful behaviour and sanctioning the hindering behaviour. You do it like this.

1. **Expect a positive response.** Use what you know about how our minds work to get into the right frame of mind about them before you talk to them. Understand that they'll pick up your thoughts about them from what your subconscious projects and make sure your thoughts are positive. If you've gone through the process in Chapters 13 and 14 you should already have a positive view. But if you haven't, don't try to fake it because they'll pick up on it, so, if you're thinking negatively about someone you need to influence deal with that before you meet them. Do that by finding the hindering beliefs that have led you to create a negative experience of them, challenging them and replacing them with something positive.

2. Make sure you're congruent. When you give out signals on a conscious and subconscious level, you need to be congruent so the other person's subconscious reading and conscious reading will be aligned. Now, if you've gone through the thinking process in Chapter 12, this will happen naturally, but if not just make sure you don't say anything you don't actually believe. Say less than you want to if you have to but say only those things you can say with total conviction and the other person will pick up your congruence.

3. Choose your responses carefully. Again, use what you know about the way our minds work to monitor your reactions to the other person. Be alert for signs that you're reacting on autopilot and, if in doubt, slow the conversation down to give yourself time to process what you're picking up. Use the considered response technique to ensure you choose the response that supports the subconscious expectations you're trying to create.

If this all sounds horribly technical and far too hard to do while trying to keep an influencing conversation going at the same time, then here's the short-cut version. Just be real. Because this technique works both ways. The three steps I've just described will result in the real you coming across clearly but, if you just focus on being real then the three steps will happen naturally as a result. And then it really is simple.

I know it sounds easier said than done but just remember, you do all this on a subconscious level already. What we're trying to do here is raise your skill level and for that you have to become conscious of the things you do subconsciously and work on them on a conscious level until you've got yourself to unconscious competence level (wow – you might need to read that again). Do you remember what it was like when you were learning to drive? And do you remember what it was like when you were able to do it without thinking? Well, it's the same here. Practise on your team if you have to but stick with it until you get it as it will single-handedly transform your performance right across the board . . . after all, you can't achieve anything in life on your own, you have to take others with you, so influencing is a core skill.

Technique 2 – influencing by asking questions

As I said, all this is going on at the same time as you're trying to have an influencing conversation and it's in the influencing conversation that we work on a conscious level using the second technique. There are only two rules:

- **Never disagree.** Or argue or make a counter-point to the points being made by the person you're trying to influence. Never, under any circumstances. Instead, listen to what they say, assume that no matter how daft or outrageous it sounds that there is a logic and ask questions until you find it.

- **Facilitate them in influencing themselves.** Use what you know about thinking being the process of asking and answering questions to ask questions that expose the flaws in their thinking. If you can see a flaw in what they're saying, don't tell them what you're seeing, think about what question you'd have to ask to get them to see it for themselves and ask it.

Remember that influencing is about changing what's in people's heads and for that to happen they have to do their own thinking. Help them think more clearly by asking better questions than they're asking themselves. Ask questions that get them to surface their beliefs and see the connection between hindering beliefs and negative experiences. Think of yourself as a catalyst for their own self-influencing process.

I can't tell you what questions to ask, only you can work that out by listening hard to what they're saying. Even if you're going in cold and didn't go through all the preceding steps, you can still use the relate-not-rapport approach to really engage with what they're saying. Don't forget – this technique applies to you as much as them, so use their questions as a way of challenging and deepening your own thinking.

IN SHORT

▶ **Our minds work in complex but fascinating ways.** Has anything you've read in this chapter changed the way you think about influencing?

▶ **We create subconscious expectations in others.** What might you do differently to improve your impact?

▶ **We think by asking and answering questions.** Have you ever experienced failing to influence someone by arguing your case then succeeding just by asking them a question?

16

How do you sustain influential relationships?

Learning from your experience for the long term

We learn from our experience whether we're conscious of it or not

When I first introduce people to the idea of regular reviews for learning, they aren't usually that keen. When overworked managers get to the end of a task they just want to get on to the next task. If things went well, they feel there's nothing to learn and if they went badly they don't want to relive them. And I feel the same way. I don't do reviews for learning because they're a good thing to do – I'm as caught up in the intensity of day-to-day work as the next person. I do them out of fear. Fear of what I might be learning if I leave it in the hands of my subconscious. Because that's the problem with not doing regular, conscious, reviews for learning. Contrary to how it might seem, the result isn't that we don't learn anything from our experience, because we always learn from our experience whether we're conscious of it or not. And we learn bad habits and hindering beliefs as easily as good habits and helpful beliefs. Let me explain that a bit more because it took me a while to get my head round it and yet it's the simple key to breaking hindering patterns of behaviour and creating better results.

Subconscious learning is a risky business

Learning starts when something happens, an event we can interpret to create an experience. We review the event, gain some insight, challenge our previous insight and apply what we've learned to our next similar experience, usually in a trial-and-error way, adjusting as we go. When we learn subconsciously we do it in a very simple way – we learn to do more of what brings us pleasure and less of what brings us pain.

Like most things to do with human nature, our **needs** are simultaneously complex and simple. Simple because we only have two core needs – avoid pain and get pleasure [or, as we get older and more sophisticated, to avoid negative consequences and seek positive consequences]. Complex because our beliefs about what causes pain and pleasure are unique to us.

But, and this is the problem, sometimes what brings us pleasure in the short term brings us pain in the longer term. Let me ask you a question. Have you ever seen someone do a bad piece of work for a frustrated boss who, rather than spend time with the team member putting him straight, just takes the problem from him and solves it himself? Now, giving the work back to the team member and getting him to do it again is painful for both of them, so it's understandable why they'd want to avoid it, but what do you think they are both learning on a subconscious level? And in case you're wondering why it matters what they learn if they're both happy with the outcome, let me remind you that our subconscious, while working hard to keep us away from pain in the short term is also programmed to ensure that if our actions are derived from hindering beliefs we create negative experiences that force us to re-examine those beliefs at some point.

Getting off to the best start for learning

One of the biggest problems in learning effectively from our experience is that we create the wrong experience in the first place through misinterpreting events. If a team member who has his mistake taken from him interprets that event as a positive experience (as in 'I got away with it') then he's going to learn something different from a team member who interprets it as a negative experience (as in 'how am I going to get any better if I'm not allowed to correct my mistakes?').

Which means getting the best interpretation

Because we interpret events through the filter of our beliefs we often don't realize there's any other way to interpret them than the one we've chosen. Yet, if we made a creative thinking exercise out of interpreting an event I bet we could come up with a lot more interpretations than just one! It's the kind of thing we've all done when we've helped a colleague or friend through a difficult experience by trying to get them to see it in a different light. All I'm suggesting is that we do it for ourselves too. Why don't you have a go now? Think about an event that happened to you recently and break it down into two elements:

■ *The things that actually happened* – that a neutral observer would have described and that would be agreed by all involved.

■ *The experience you created of those events* – the way you interpreted them that led you to judge them as positive or negative.

Now think about how many other ways you could have interpreted it. And think about what you have to believe about yourself, other people and the world at large to interpret it the way you first did. Now, I'm not saying for a minute that you interpreted it wrongly in the first place, I'm just trying to demonstrate that

Ask what you're teaching the other person through their experience of you.

we have choices and that learning works better when we make those choices consciously rather than subconsciously. You might still decide your original interpretation was the most helpful one for you but how much more confidence does it give you to know that you ran it through the 'consciousness' test and it passed with flying colours.

It's not just you who learns from your relationships

While we're on the subject of sustaining good-quality two-way influencing relationships I need to remind you that it's not just you who learns from them. Ask yourself what you're teaching the other person through their experience of you. Are they learning to treat you with respect and not to manipulate you? Are they learning that you have principles and limits? Are they learning that your relationship with them is important to you and that you respect them? Why not use your imagination to help you work out what kind of experience of you they might be creating from the events that have taken place in your relationship?

I prefer **imagination** to **empathy** because empathy is so easy to get wrong. Too often people think empathy is about how we'd feel if we were in someone else's situation. But we get it wrong because we take our own frame of reference with us whereas, if we actually were in their situation, we'd be looking from a different perspective so we'd feel and do things differently. Getting this wrong is often what stops us understanding people.

Two final thoughts

A management skills book on influencing is duty bound to focus on influencing as a specific manageable process. But as we draw the process to a close before moving on to advice on how to get the process back on track when it hits problems, I'd like to leave you with two thoughts to put the influencing process in context:

■ Influencing is so much more than just how to get people to do what we want. For one thing, our significant relationships influence us deeply whether we're conscious of it or not. That's an obvious thing to say when you think about life and the people we love but remember we spend a lot of time at work with colleagues who can make a big difference to our experience of work so it applies there too.

■ Influencing is only hard work when we aren't true to ourselves, when we aren't real with people. We influence people by who we are, by the way they experience us. If we try to be something we're not, if we say one thing and do another, if we put our relationships or the task ahead of our principles, we won't succeed in influencing people no matter how many clever techniques we know (ask any spin doctor).

IN SHORT

▶ **We can learn consciously or subconsciously but we always learn something.** How much of what you learn is subconscious?

▶ **We create our experience through our interpretation of events.** Have you ever interpreted things one way at the time of the event only to change your interpretation later on?

▶ **We teach people about us from the way we treat them.** What do you think the people you're influencing are learning about you?

PART 3

■ *real* management for the way it is ■

Knowing when you need to adjust your approach

▶ **Noticing when things aren't going according to plan**

The process I've just described is what would happen in an ideal world, where each step works well and no one throws a spanner in the works. I wrote it like that because influencing is a complex process and I wanted to explain it as simply as possible. But we live in the real world where people do throw spanners in the works so this part of the book looks at the things that can go wrong and gives you some ideas for how you can get things back on track.

▶ **Don't just take my word for it . . . check it against your own experience**

As you read this part think back to your last experience of influencing and review it against what you're reading.

17

When can't you get them to listen?

The need to establish credibility and get their undivided attention

Is it me or is it them?

The harsh reality is that there are some people with whom we're never going to have credibility but that says more about them than us. People who won't listen to us because we're male, female, black, white, short, tall, thin, fat, young, old, red-haired, blond-haired, whatever. That reality makes it tempting, whenever we're having trouble establishing our credibility, to make it the other person's problem. But I think we all know when something is a one-off and when it's a pattern. And if it's the latter, then maybe we're the common denominator and it's a sign that we need to take a long hard look at our credibility.

Using your experience as a lever for change

One of the best things about learning from experience is that we have so much experience to learn from. For example, I'm sure we've all been on both sides of the divide I'm dealing with in this chapter many times before. I mean, we've not just experienced not being able to get to first base with people, we've also experienced being the one that can't be persuaded even to listen.

I believe our strongest intentions win the day so if we want to be credible and influential with people we need to do two things:

- Be very clear about what 'being credible' and 'being influential' is.

- Be absolutely sure it's what we really want.

Let me say something on that second point before we focus the rest of the chapter on the first point. For a long time, I kept having this déjà vu experience of people not listening to me at a time when it could have helped them and then, when it's too late, they'd come to me and say they wished they'd listened. I couldn't understand it. Being listened to was very important to me as a person, not just in my job, yet it was the one thing I couldn't seem to achieve. And I knew it was me because it was happening too often for me to dismiss it as other people's problem. I tried different techniques but nothing helped.

Eventually, I realized I needed to apply the philosophy I used to coach people to my own situation so I asked myself what I had to gain from people *not* listening to me. And that's when I found my stronger, and conflicting, intention – I didn't want to feel responsible for other people's actions and when they acted on my advice, I blamed myself if things went wrong even though I knew (on a conscious level) that it wasn't my fault. So, before we move on, go back to Chapter 9 and remind yourself of your answer to my question about what you have to gain when your influencing goes wrong.

Knowing what makes someone credible and influential

I can (and will) tell you what I think but what's important is what makes sense to you, so let's start there. Think about someone you know well who's influenced you in the past, someone you'd describe as credible and influential. Now, analyze their performance and identify their characteristics. Start by thinking about what they actually did. If you want to use my list as a prompt, I'm influenced by people who:

- know what they're talking about
- are straight with me and don't try to manipulate me
- don't try to impose their views on me
- speak with conviction and enthusiasm about what matters to them
- don't belittle my concerns or patronize me for having them
- are honest with me and don't avoid the difficult issues
- don't make promises they can't keep
- take responsibility for their actions (and inactions)
- think about my questions and don't just trot out answers they baked earlier
- take on board things I say and are influenced by me
- I have a good general relationship with
- I trust.

Does my list look anything like yours? OK, now to get a more rounded picture, I want you to think about someone who doesn't have any credibility or influence with you. What are their characteristics? Is it just the opposite of your first list or does analyzing their performance shed some new light on the subject? Asking you that question has triggered thoughts in my mind of some of my most empty experiences of credibility and influence. Surprisingly enough, they come from watching motivational speakers who command small fortunes for their services. As someone who loves words, I know that listening to great words spoken by a great speaker can be a very powerful experience. I've been to lots of such sessions and I always come away fired up and determined to change but I never seem to follow it up. As the old saying has it, I'm all dressed up with nowhere to go.

I suspect that, of all the things powerful orators achieve, real influence isn't one of them. I think real influence comes from the way people behave with us on a day-to-day basis. I think we sometimes ascribe influence to people whose words we feel have had an impact on us but I think what they've done is not persuade us so much as struck a chord with something we already knew on a subconscious level. A skill in its own right, yes, but a different skill to influencing.

Credible, influential people sweat the small stuff

We're told not to sweat the small stuff and yet, when you think about it, it's the people who sweat the small stuff who have real influence over us. The people who behave in trustworthy, honourable ways all the time and not just when they want something from us.

Because it's a state of being not an act of doing

Of course influencing includes things you do but I define it as a state of being, a state of mind, because that's where the things we do come from – our thoughts. We all have the capacity to do the right thing in the recognizably big moments in our lives because we can pause, consider and weigh up the options but on a moment-by-moment, choice-by-choice basis, we tend to react on autopilot and that's how people know if our credibility is real and not a mask.

A **mask** is something we pretend we are, to cover something we are pretending we aren't. I have an arrogant streak I don't much like so I wear the mask of openness about things I'm not good at. It has a positive effect on others [they become open too] so I think of my mask as the positive side of my arrogant streak.

Establishing credibility with someone new

Having said all that, we all still have occasions when we need to establish credibility quickly with someone who doesn't know us. So, what do you do? Four things:

■ *Don't try* – paradoxically enough, the best thing you can do to establish your credibility is not to even try to do it. People who try really hard to establish their credibility often suffer from what I call the 'protesting too much' reaction. This is where the harder you try to be credible the more people think it's a way of hiding the fact that you're not.

■ *Focus on them* – two reasons for this. First, if you remember the pink elephant example, it's hard to focus on not doing something but it's easy to replace it with focusing on something else. Second, if you analyze the person you're trying to influence it will help you find the way in, the hook that gets them to listen to you.

- *Say things they want to listen to* – unsurprisingly, I've never had any trouble getting anyone to listen to me when I'm talking about them so I make sure I say a lot of things they want to hear first (only things I can say in all honesty, of course) so I can establish a listening environment that will, hopefully, sustain itself when the subject matter changes.

- *Reward the behaviour you want* – remember how people learn by trial and error (do something, get feedback, adjust, get more feedback)? Well, make sure they're learning the right things by letting them know when they do something you like (such as hear you out without interrupting).

Finding the hook that gets their undivided attention

Getting someone to listen is largely about saying something that makes them want to hear more. And that something is different for every person. If you've focused on them, as I suggest in the previous paragraph, you should have gleaned enough information about them to find the perfect hook.

Think about what's in it for them. Think about how you can trigger what they already know at subconscious level – an incisive question can be a brilliant hook. Think about working with them at belief level by asking yourself what someone would have to believe (about themselves, other people, the world at large) to agree with your proposal. Think about what they might be dissatisfied with, because influence is about changing what's in people's heads so it helps to know what they might be most willing to change.

IN SHORT

▶ **Credible is as credible does.** If I asked the people who work with you how credible you are, what would they say?

▶ **If you can't describe it, you can't be it.** What, in your view, is the most essential characteristic for credibility?

▶ **If you want to get someone's attention, you need a hook.** How effective are you at getting people to listen?

18

When have they listened but rejected you?

The need to learn from your experience and adjust-as-you-go

Understand what's happening

So, you've made your case, written your report, done your presentation, whatever, and it's not having the desired effect. Time for a review for learning. Start by doing a normal review for learning on your own performance to gain some insight that will help you adjust your approach. Then, ask the normal review for learning questions about their performance so you gain some insight about what parts of their response you need to change.

I know that's going to be a challenge – especially as you may feel there was nothing in their response that was at all helpful but remember that nothing is ever 100 per cent one way or the other, so keep looking. It's only natural that, if you've come out of a dismal encounter feeling like you've made no progress at all, you won't see anything that counters your judgement (you know the lengths our subconscious will go to, to keep us thinking we're right). It's natural, but it's not helpful, so get out of judging mode by getting into neutral analyzing mode.

Separate events from interpretations and expectations

When you're doing your review for learning, make sure your analysis separates out what actually happened from how you interpreted it to create your experience then challenge your interpretation. Bear in mind that often we're disappointed in an outcome because we had unrealistic expectations. Maybe what you're interpreting as the person not listening is actually just them being not as enthusiastic and instantly won over as you'd expected. Extroverts are often disappointed in the reaction of introverts who may prefer to mull things over after they've gone before making their minds up and whose neutrality may appear negative.

In a short chapter, I can't list all the things that might possibly have gone wrong and, even if I could, it would defeat the object as you need to be on manual to make this work and if I did your thinking for you, you'd be on autopilot. What I can do though, is offer you some places where you can look for answers during your analysis.

Check you're not objectifying them

People react to a stimulus and though it's perfectly possible there's some kind of displacement going on (they're taking out on you their feelings about something or someone else) let's rule out the more likely explanation first – that it was something you did or said that triggered their response.

The biggest thing that switches people off is the feeling that they're just a target.

The biggest thing that switches people off when we're trying to influence them is the feeling that they're just a target, not a person in their own right. So check you're not treating them like an object. Are you using the same approach with every-one? By the same token, check you're not adapting your approach in inappropriate ways – like talking down to front-line staff. To check you've focused enough on them, make a list of everything you've learned about them. If it's a short list then maybe you haven't been seeing them as real and complex people.

Check you're the right person to be doing the influencing

You can only have real influence with the circle of people with whom you interact regularly so don't assume you'll be able to influence people who don't know you. Do you know the John Guare play *Six Degrees of Separation*? I saw the movie version with Stockard Channing, Donald Sutherland and Will Smith (brilliant). The premise of the play is that we're all connected to each other by six or fewer stages of circumstance or acquaintance. So, if you're not the right person to be doing the influencing, use the six degrees of separation idea to get the people you have influence with to influence the people they have influence with and so on.

While we're on the subject, you might want to think about this as a strategic approach to influencing. Most senior man-agers trying to influence organizational change do it within the hierarchy in top-down fashion. That approach assumes the people over whom we have influence are the same people over whom we have authority. If only. So, think about mobilizing your organization's six degrees of separa-tion. And if you're planning to use this method regularly, it's worth investing in teaching your staff influencing skills

Get the people you have influence with to influence the people they have influence with.

because youdon't want them thinking that what won them over will win other people over.

Check you're trying to influence, not get your own way

Getting your own way may feel like the ultimate form of influence but there's a big difference between the two. If you get your own way, the chances are that people will slip back unless you're constantly topping them up. Real influence is self-sustainable, because you've changed what's in people's heads. So, when you analyze your performance, make sure you check this point. You can do it by listing all the things they said or did that influenced you and changed what's in your head. If there's nothing to list, chances are you were in get-your-own-way mode rather than two-way influencing mode.

Check your relationship is sound

Sometimes our proposals are rejected because they ask too much of our relationship. In my story in Part 1 with my team, I realize now that I was asking people who hardly knew me to accept my approach. If you're going to ask people to have faith in you, you'd best have a strong relationship to back it up. So, did you follow the steps in the influencing process in Part 2 or did you just leap straight into the techniques in Chapter 15 and hope for the best. Well, those techniques will often work on their own but if the proposals are asking for a big change of mind then success will be more dependent on the state of your relationship than the quality of your influencing techniques.

So, do a health check on this and if you think that's where the problem lies, put the issue on one side and put the time into building a two-way influencing relationship.

Check your proposals are attractive

Being rejected is an uncomfortably paradoxical experience. Most human beings (and people who say differently are in denial) take rejection personally but cope with it by working as if it were the request or proposal that was rejected. I've put this paragraph last because, in my experience, it's never about the actual proposals but it's worth looking at them not for their overt content but for their covert content. In other words, for what they tell someone about you.

Being rejected is an uncomfortably paradoxical experience.

Read them through and imagine they were written by someone you've never met. What are they telling you about the person who developed them? Are they self-absorbed or inclusive? Are they open to being influenced or bent on getting their own way?

Only you know how to apply your insight

I've focused in this chapter on helping you gain some useful insight into why your proposals were rejected rather than on what you can do to reverse the situation. That's because the 'putting things right' bit is so dependent on all the variables we talked about in Chapter 10 that it would be impossible for me to give you techniques for every situation. So, it's down to you. Do your analysis, gain your insight, do something different, listen and watch for feedback and adjust as you go and you'll get there.

IN SHORT

▶ **Rejection is the perfect opportunity to learn from experience.** How often do you review specific interactions with people and your relationships in general?

▶ **Beware unrealistic expectations.** If you reviewed your experience the last time you were disappointed, would you say your expectations were realistic?

▶ **Develop a real circle of influence.** Could you list the people in your department with whom you have influence and those with whom you do not?

19

When does it seem to have descended into an argument?

The need to challenge perspectives and expectations, especially your own

When influencing becomes arguing

Wouldn't life be lovely if all our attempts to influence people blossomed into two-way influencing relationships? Sadly, in real life, they often descend into conflict and argument.

Arguing is always personal

I remember being on a behavioural analysis course where the trainer was distinguishing between behaviour that consisted of two people disagreeing with each other and behaviour that was an attack/defend spiral. He said attack/defend behaviour was personal and disagreement was issue based, not personal. This is naïve – in real life, people feel ownership of things they've produced or issues they've supported and if you speak against their stuff they may well feel you're attacking them.

But it's also a chance to make transformational progress

It's only natural that when we start to lock horns with someone we become focused on winning the battle not the hearts and minds. Natural but not helpful. This is more than ever the time when you need to focus on your principles and not get sidetracked by reacting to whatever they're throwing at you. Remember, that's why you took the time to get your own clarity in the first place – so you wouldn't end up getting tossed and blown about by other people's reactions. Still, all this is easier said than done so give yourself a break – literally – while you work out what to do next.

Breaking our natural response cycle

You probably know already that we have a natural response cycle. It goes something like this:

- Something happens to stimulate a response – we see, hear, touch, taste or smell something or a combination of those things.

- We process the stimulus – against all the information that's stored in our subconscious (like a computer checking fingerprints for a match, only faster).

- We find an experience of a similar stimulus and we locate the pre-programmed response that goes with it (that came from the way we responded to that stimulus last time).

- We make our response.

- We get feedback on our response from whoever we responded to (and possibly from others in the vicinity). This response then becomes our stimulus for our next response.

And so the cycle continues. The fact that our natural response cycle runs on autopilot at a rate faster than the speed of light is very handy when we're in a life and death situation but it's not that handy when we're in an argument – because we can have made the situation ten times worse before we've even realized what we've done. So, take a deep breath and put a pause between stimulus and response.

Use the pause to challenge your assumptions and expectations

An argument implies a conflict. And a conflict implies a hindering belief, because all negative experiences (which is how most of us see conflict) can be tracked back to hindering beliefs. Now, I know this is a book all about changing what's in other people's heads but at this point in the proceedings the only viable way forward is to change what's in *your* head. So, start by getting your position clear in your own mind. Now, ask yourself what must someone believe to take that position. It may feel strange to analyze yourself as if you were a neutral observer but try to be as detached as you can. Once you've found all your beliefs, put them up for the Two Rs Challenge – realistic and reasonable – and see which ones need to change. Looking for the evidence that the hindering belief causes the negative experience will help you find the motivation to choose a more helpful belief and thinking about what kind of experience you'd like to create will help you find a new belief to put in its place.

An argument implies a conflict. And a conflict implies a hindering belief.

Then choose a better response

This is the considered-response variation of our natural response. Have you regretted a knee-jerk response recently? Well, get some positive mileage out of it by putting it through the following four questions.

1. *What was the stimulus and is there any other way of interpreting it than the way I interpreted it?* There is always more than one way of interpreting an event so come up with as many different ways as you can and then carefully select the one that makes most sense.

2. *What do I want to achieve with my response and will my natural reaction get me that?* The trouble with our natural response is that it's reactive, so it relates purely to the stimulus and not to the effect we want to achieve. So, use the pause to think about what effect you want your response to achieve and to see whether your natural reaction will achieve it.

3. *What other options for responding do I have?* Now shift from reactive to proactive and come up with alternative options.

4. *Which option gets me everything I need and makes common sense (appealing both to the logic of my conscious mind and the intuition of my subconscious mind)?* And now we're into decision-making mode. Weighing up the options and selecting the appropriate response.

So, how was it for you? Did you come up with a better response to your recent knee-jerk example?

Because changing your response changes the dynamic

As you know, I believe the first step in any process is to understand the dynamic way the variables in that process interact.

Well, this chapter – with its focus on changing your perspective and response to change the dynamic – shows why I think the way I do.

IN SHORT

▶ **Conflict is an opportunity for transformational progress.**
Have you ever snatched victory from the jaws of defeat?

▶ **When things go wrong, look at yourself first.** Where do you look first, at yourself or the other person?

▶ **Respond, don't react.** Have you ever got into a negative spiral by matching fire with fire when you should have been taking the heat out of the situation?

20

When are they trying to manipulate you?

The need to recognize and manage the games people play

Not all your problems will be open ones

In the last chapter, we talked about managing your way through open problems. But what about when people don't openly argue with you or attack your position, but try to con you into giving them what they want?

There are lots of games out there – playing one person off against another, saying what you want to hear then doing something different or doing nothing at all, using the idea of playing devil's advocate as a cover for taking pot shots at you, knowing they have something you want and enjoying making you jump through hoops. I'm sure you can add lots more examples to that list but the point is, it doesn't matter what the game is, it matters how you respond.

Judge the game, not the person playing it

Before you leap into judgement about people who play games, remember they aren't always doing it consciously – games are one of the many ways our creative subconscious keeps us sane and we all play them. It doesn't make us bad people. And some people genuinely believe they're being real with you. It may well be something you've sensed as an incongruence but they haven't registered at all – because their RAS doesn't let them. Some of the nicest people I know are people pleasers with a strong need to be liked and they often find themselves in situations where they say what people want to hear rather than what they really think. It's a game, in the sense that everything that isn't real is a game, but they can't see it.

Don't inadvertently reward people for unacceptable behaviour

People who play games do it because they've learned they work. And they work because often, without even realizing we're doing it, we play along with their games and give them what they need. It's true what the psychologists say – we get the behaviour we reward. I knew someone once who was a macho control freak who thought having needs was a sign of weakness. To get what he wanted without having to own up to having a need, he'd learned, over **People who play games do it because they've learned they work.** the years, to play mind games that wouldn't be out of place on a Derren Brown show. Now, I've always believed that people who play games are essentially fear driven, so I tend to feel sorry for them. A typical interaction would go something like this. He'd try to manipulate me into doing something for him which I didn't need to be manipulated into doing because I'd have been happy to do it anyway so all he needed to do was ask. But I knew he didn't feel he could ask so I made allowances and gave him what he needed anyway. At the time, I figured I was doing the right thing but it wasn't until he started manipulating me into doing things that went against my principles that I realized I'd created in him an expectation that manipulating me was okay.

When you're trying to influence someone who plays games you need to accept that you have to do your influencing on two levels – the issue and their behaviour. Because, if you go along with their games you're, in effect, encouraging them to keep playing them and you'll never develop a two-way influencing relationship.

Respond to the person, don't react to the game

OK, so much for what not to do, the first proactive thing to do in dealing with people who play games is to set clear boundaries so you can respond to the person rather than react to their game. Why? Because if you let someone push you into reacting in a way that undermines your objective, you're lost before you've even begun. Decide what you will and won't put up with. This will be easy if you did the work in Chapter 12 on principles because your principles will determine your boundaries.

And bring them back to adult/adult mode

When people play games they're either acting like children or parents (depending on the game) and a successful two-way influencing relationship requires an adult/adult relationship. You don't have to be a parent to know that it's pretty difficult when someone is acting like a child not to automatically respond like a parent. That's how suggestible our subconscious mind is – it picks up the vibes being given off by the person playing the game and wants to respond in kind.

In the last chapter, we talked about the value of pausing to reflect and to give a considered response when there is argument and conflict. Well, the same applies to games and manipulation attempts. You need to pause – it doesn't have to be for more than the time it takes to count to ten – and choose to respond as an adult. What helps me in this situation is to reflect on what they've said or done and think about how they might have said it if they'd not been playing games – if they'd been behaving as an adult. Then I use the listening to articulate technique to translate what they've said into game-free, adult/adult language, check I've understood them correctly and then respond.

Listening to articulate the reality behind the game

I have a relative who's always broke and sponging off the rest of the family but who's never directly asked anyone for money, ever. Here's how she does it. She rings up in tears to tell me the latest sob story about her finances, a story that always ends with I need x amount of money by y date and I just don't know where I'm going to get it. I used to just offer the money which, of course, rewarded the behaviour and led me to resent her but now I say 'are you asking me if I'll lend you some money because if you are, I'm happy to' which means that if she wants to have her need met, she has to acknowledge it in an adult way and drop the game.

What we're doing when we respond like this is working with the game player on a number of levels. On one level, we're calling their bluff on their game, making them bring their need out in the open. On another level, we're teaching them that playing games doesn't work with us. And on yet another level, we're recognizing and responding to the fact that they only play the game because they're afraid of being straight with us about their need. How did we do that? By ending the sentence in which we translated their game into something real with a reassurance that we will meet their need.

Going back to basics

There's a limit to how much you can use techniques to manage the games people play so I want to end this chapter with a reminder that in the end there are only two things you can do. You can confront the issue and work on building a game-free relationship – which means going back to the last chapter and dealing with the cause of the conflict – or you can give up, and that's the next chapter.

IN SHORT

▶ **Everyone plays games, but not always consciously.** What games do other people play that really push your buttons and would a trusted colleague say you play the same ones?

▶ **Be careful what behaviour you reward.** Do you ever inadvertently reward behaviour that is unacceptable?

▶ **Don't let them drag you into their game.** How do you react to other people's games, with games of your own?

21

When does the substantive issue threaten the relationship?

The need to value your principles and know when to walk away

When the sacrifice is too great

When trying to influence others, it may happen that you feel so strongly about an issue (because a principle is violated) that it threatens the whole relationship. It may have arisen out of the conflict and argument we discussed in Chapter 19 or from the gamesmanship in Chapter 20 but whatever the cause, the relationship has reached a crisis point. And it's important that we respect the crisis for what it is – because people come and go at work and in our lives but we carry our conscience with us wherever we are. And we only have a clear conscience when we put our principles first.

Too much pressure on managers

Managers are under increasing pressure these days to do the expedient thing rather than the right thing. When I look back over my career, I'm most proud of the fact that I managed to have good relationships with unions and managers during a period of industrial relations history where there was immense pressure from central government on the public sector to sideline the unions. And I did it without compromising my principles. But I know managers who didn't and who ended up losing their self-respect.

We all need something to guide our decisions at work, something that matters more to us than our working relationships, our goals, our careers even. Our principles are the basis against which we compare (whether consciously or subconsciously) our day-to-day behaviour and judge ourselves – so they have a massive effect on our self-esteem. Besides, what's the alternative? Being liked? I think we all know how transient that is.

Living by your principles is an act of courage

Whether you walk away from a destructive working relationship or stay and sort it out, it's an act of courage to say 'enough, we can't go on this way' even if you only say it to yourself because the person on the other end of the relationship is your boss or a valued client. Sometimes putting up with things we know are unacceptable seems like the only option, but there's always a price to pay in the end when we aren't true to ourselves because our subconscious creates negative experiences to challenge us to face reality.

Way back in Chapter 2 I talked about being happy in a healthy way both with yourself and the results you create. Well, that's what suffers when you put a relationship above your principles, when you're not true to yourself in your dealings with people, when you have to live with the grinding, day-to-day stress of pretending to be someone you're not.

But let's not get dogmatic about it

Of course, before you walk away from an important relationship, you need to examine its value and assess which of your principles it's undermining and the value of that principle to you. But you also need to reassess your principles because we can have principles we haven't challenged in years and have maybe outgrown.

Everyone has to decide for themselves what principles are right for them – what I'm saying here is that you need to have challenged the validity of your principles. This is not about moral absolutes or rigid principles or being pious or pompous with people – it's about knowing what matters most to you, knowing what you stand for. And it's not about making the people you have relationships with feel less important than your principles. On the contrary, when you have clear principles they support your relationships. They make it easier for people to read you, to predict your responses and they trust you because they know where they stand with you.

You need to have challenged the validity of your principles.

Every crisis is also an opportunity

The upside of finding a substantive issue that threatens to tear a relationship apart is that it gives you the biggest incentive you'll ever have for doing a wholesale review of the relationship and taking action to make it stronger.

Working on the relationship is one option

If you've decided the relationship is important to you then this is the obvious option. Now, there are literally thousands of books out there on making successful relationships and their messages apply as much to working relationships as to personal ones. To be honest, though, I find most relationship-building books a bit touchy-feely for me. When I have a problem with a relationship, I prefer to solve it the way I would solve any other problem. I list all the problems (the unwanted effects, the things that don't work) and I determine the cause of each problem. Then I keep asking what causes that problem until I track back to the single root cause and then I focus all my energy on solving that. I know it sounds a bit too rational a method for dealing with interpersonal problems but I've helped many friends over the years deal with all sorts of emotional problems using this method and it's not only solved the problem, it's also improved their emotional state because it's taken the heat out of the situation. Now I know you have your preferred method of solving problems so what I'm really saying is why not use it for relationship and people problems. You might surprise yourself with the results.

Walking away (literally or figuratively) is another

This is the option if you've decided the relationship isn't important to you. Sometimes we can literally walk away (by getting another job for example) and sometimes, because the person is the boss and finding another job isn't possible, we can only walk away figuratively. Walking away doesn't mean you won't be able to work with someone again, it just means you'll handle the relationship differently.

Walking away doesn't mean you won't be able to work with someone again, it just means you'll handle the relationship differently.

I remember joining an organization once and being seen as a threat by a colleague who clearly felt the creation of my post threatened the future of his. I tried hard for a long time to build a relationship with him but he wouldn't have a bar of it. And when he stabbed me in the back with our boss for the second time, I decided I didn't need him so I walked away. From that day, I was polite, I always kept him informed, I did what a good colleague would do. But it was all surface stuff, there was no trust. It didn't affect my work and it didn't affect my job satisfaction.

On another occasion, though, when my relationship with my then boss collapsed over a point of principle, I couldn't walk away figuratively because it can't be done in a relationship between a manager and her boss. So I found another job and walked away literally. The sense of release, after months of trying to make the relationship work and compromising every principle that mattered to me, was enormous.

Which can be temporary or permanent

Sometimes people just need time. You've said how you feel and what's important to you. You've established your boundaries and been clear about what you will and won't put up with but remember, it's their insight that influences them not yours. And people often need time to process their insight. So you just have to get on with things and wait until they've sorted themselves out.

Learning from your experience

Whatever you decide to do, make it work for you by learning from your experience. In your reviews for learning, ask yourself what you would have done differently if you had the time over and use that insight in managing your relationships in the future.

IN SHORT

▶ **Principles have to come before relationships.** Have you ever experienced sacrificing a principle for a relationship only to resent if afterwards?

▶ **Challenge your principles on a regular basis.** How often do you review your principles to see if they're still the ones you want to live by?

▶ **Know when to stay and when to walk.** How do you manage relationships with people at work after irrevocable damage has been done?

22

When are they committed but afraid to take the plunge?

The need to help people work through their fears and emotions

It takes a brave person to admit they're scared

I'm sure we all have experience of being committed to a change yet still being concerned about what that change might mean for us. It's tempting, once you've influenced people to think that's an end to it but it's not. Even when you've changed what's in their heads, the people you've influenced may still need support to face their fears and to turn the changes in their heads into changes in their behaviour.

Take their feelings seriously

People in the throes of personal change will often have periods of discouragement. Help them by suspending your judgement and starting from where they are. It doesn't matter whether you think they're exaggerating or distorting because if they believe they've got a problem, they've got a problem. Take their emotions as fact and help them solve the problem that's causing them to think that way. Once they're focused on that, they'll feel more positive. As you listen, try not to inadvertently invalidate their emotions. It's easily done. Think about the last time you felt discouraged only to hear people say 'You can do it' or 'It's not that bad'. Well, when you think about it, they're saying, 'You're wrong to think or feel the way you do.'

Help them deal with their fears

The more successful you've been in changing what's in people's heads the more tempted they can be to ignore their fears. Don't let that happen. Our fears will make themselves known so if we don't listen to them on a conscious level, our subconscious will listen anyway and will engineer ways of sabotaging their commitment to change. Use the techniques in this book to help them surface their fears and work though them.

Rehearse new ways of working

You may well have dealt with a number of hindering beliefs during the earlier parts of the influencing process – especially if you had to deal with conflict or games – but some hindering beliefs will only surface once you've got their commitment. Help people see the connection between their hindering beliefs, their behaviours and their results. Then help them think about the results they'd like to achieve and the beliefs that would deliver those results. One of the best ways to do this is to do a 'walkthrough' of the new ways of working.

A **'walkthrough'** is just when someone rehearses an event in their head by describing, in storytelling detail, what is happening from start to finish. It's a bit like doing a running radio commentary on a fantasy football match, if you'll pardon the metaphor. One person describes what's happening and the others ask questions to make sure no details get missed. You have to remember to keep asking questions of the 'where's the ref at this point?' kind so you are sure nothing and no one gets missed. It's sounds weird but it's great for anticipating potential problems.

Use the discussion of how things will be in the future to flush out any areas of uncertainty or negativity and ask questions to uncover underlying fears and hindering beliefs and to challenge them.

Give them what they need

When someone changes what's in their heads, it's change at a fundamental and deeply personal level. The knock-on effect is enormous and it takes time for them to come to terms with that. But we all come to terms with things in different ways and we need different types of support at different times. Don't assume that other people are like you so ask them what support they need from you.

Follow up

It may be that after your first post-influencing intervention, all goes well, but don't take that for granted. If you're developing a two-way influencing relationship with people then you will still be having regular contact, so use that to keep an eye on how things are going.

IN SHORT

▶ **Don't stop influencing just because they've signed up.**
Have you ever thought you'd done the job only to find
things slipping back when you looked the other way?

▶ **Treat emotional problems like any other problem.** Have
you ever inadvertently dismissed someone's fears or
invalidated their emotions?

■ *real* management for the way it is ■

Conclusion

▶ **Leaving the hard sell until last**

I think almost every book I've read on influencing starts by selling you the benefits, presumably to motivate you to actually try influencing. It seems more logical to me to assume that you're already motivated to want to try influencing otherwise you wouldn't have bought the book.

▶ **Do you want the benefits enough to face up to the complexity?**

Not sure? Then read on . . .

23

Why should you persevere with *real* influencing when it's so complex?

I can't answer that, I can only tell you why I persevere

Only you know why you bought this book and what it would take to motivate you to try some of the ideas I'm putting forward. All I can do is tell you what motivates me to persevere with real influencing and what I get out of it.

Without *real* influence, you can't achieve anything

The whole idea of management being the art of making things happen through other people highlights just how important influencing skills are. As a manager I know I can't achieve anything without the co-operation of other people and that means knowing how to influence them.

It's the best stress reduction technique I know

Although I've talked in this book a lot about process and techniques, I hope you've seen that all I've been doing with those processes and techniques is describe what happens when

Most of the stress we come under at work comes from having to be something we're not.

people are real with each other. Because the key to real influencing is, quite simply, being real. Except it's not so simple is it? Most of the stress we come under at work comes from having to be something we're not. I've spent a lot of time developing ways of managing that allow people to be real because I know that it's the only way we can eliminate stress at work at source.

It leaves people feeling good

We all know what it's like to be on the receiving end of someone's hard sell. They're plugged in, switched on and going for it on full throttle and you're just along for the ride. It leaves me feeling like a non-person because it's clear it's not me who matters, it's what they want from me. In contrast, being part of a two-way influencing relationship leaves me feeling good – about the other person of course but, perhaps even more importantly, about myself. And we all need that.

It puts an end to the games people play

I know I shouldn't criticize because I know I play my fair share of games but I don't much like working in organizations that rely on the two-faced method of inter-personal relationships.

It really works

When I think of my attempts over the years to influence people by trying to persuade them of the rightness of my position or by arguing the flaws in theirs, I can't believe it took me so long to change to the real influencing approach. I'm not saying I had no success with the other methods – but it's nothing compared to the impact you have when you change what's in someone's head.

You don't have to feel responsible for other people

For someone with a bit of a phobia about being responsible for other people, the thing I like most about real influencing is that you're not the influencer so much as the catalyst for people to influence themselves. When you influence by asking questions, for example, the answer comes from them not from you and you know they're changing what's in their heads themselves so it's not down to you.

It changes the culture in the team

There's something refreshingly different about the dynamic in a team where the manager manages by influencing rather than by exerting authority or pulling rank. I'd be the first to admit that patience is not one of my virtues and yet I have no trouble finding the patience to help people change what's in their head even though it would be quicker just to pull rank. That's because it's a satisfying way of working.

It's a chance to hone your questioning skills

All the skills a real manager needs, but especially influencing, depend for their success on the core skill of being able to ask the right questions. It's a skill most people take for granted yet when you think about it, our education system teaches us how to answer questions but not how to ask them. And the books and courses on questioning tell you about all the different types of questions but they don't tell you how you know if you're asking the right question or how to find the one incisive question that will unlock the situation you're in. If you resist the temptation to get your own way and put your time and effort into finding the questions that will change what's in people's heads . . . you'll be a great influencer and a great manager.

All the skills a *real* manager needs, depend for their success on the core skill of being able to ask the right questions.

Appendix

Towards a way of managing for the new era

The beliefs that help me make sense of my world and the people in it, including me

Beliefs come before action – and inaction

Columbus had to believe the earth was round before he could set sail to prove it, and the same applies to us in everything we do.

People do what makes sense – even when you can't tell from their results

How many times have you reacted to someone's actions with 'But that doesn't make any sense'? We can believe human beings are irrational, or we can believe they do what makes sense but that everyone's 'sense' is different. It's easier to make sense of what people are doing if we stop thinking our logic is *the* logic. Have you ever wondered why you did something that got the opposite effect to what you wanted, even though you knew all along what would happen?

If we were conscious of everything we know, our logic would be clearer to us

Sometimes, a new experience that has similarities to an earlier experience will trigger something from the vast store of experiences we keep in our subconscious. When we do this with people, it's prejudice – literally prejudging them based on previous experience that might or might not be relevant. Have you ever taken an instant dislike to someone, then, when you got to know them, liked them? What triggered your initial response? Did they remind you of someone else you didn't like?

Our subconscious mind alerts us through our intuition

When our subconscious mind wants to tell us there's something we've forgotten that's relevant to the situation we're currently in, it uses our intuition. Have you ever listened to someone saying something that sounded logical that you still felt absolutely sure was wrong yet couldn't explain how or why?

Except when it skips that step and drives us straight to a knee-jerk action

Taking an instant dislike to someone is an example of our subconscious bypassing the intuition alert stage and driving us straight to a response. When our responses don't seem logical to our conscious minds, we fear being irrational. But as I said, people always have a logic – it just isn't always a conscious logic!

We don't fail, we just achieve an intention we didn't know we had

Have you ever tried to give up a bad habit and failed? Did you blame lack of will-power? If your conscious and subconscious minds have conflicting intentions, your subconscious will win because it's stronger. What might you have to gain from not giving up your bad habit? Or what might you have to lose from giving it up?

Our needs drive our intentions and our beliefs drive our behaviour

Our beliefs tell us how to behave to meet our needs. Like everything else we've ever learned, we learn our beliefs from our experience. What are you not doing that you know you should because you believe it will be a painful experience?

Our experience is created by our subconscious

There's a lot of rubbish talked about people creating their disability, which is a hurtful mistake people make who don't realize there's a difference between an event and an experience. Have you known two people who were at the same meeting (event) to describe it so differently (experience) that it was as if they'd been to different meetings?

Which always has its own logic – even when we can't see it

One of the main functions of our subconscious is to keep us feeling sane. The lengths it will go to is probably why it's often called the creative subconscious – as in creative accounting maybe! It governs everything, from the things we notice in the first place – have you ever bought a new car only to start seeing that model everywhere you go? – to the way we interpret events to create our experience.

Our logic comes from our beliefs

My logic will make sense to you only if we both believe that the same (a) causes the same (b). If you believe that smoking causes lung cancer but I believe there's no connection, then we'll never agree on why there's rising incidence of lung cancer among people in developing-world countries who are encouraged to smoke by unrestricted advertising practices, because we'll be analyzing using different logics.

Our ingrained beliefs stem from childhood experiences of pain and pleasure

We form many of our beliefs in childhood, which is a pity because that's when we're worst equipped to interpret events. For one thing, we're dependent on our parents to meet our needs, which means we learn to associate pleasure and pain with how they react to the way we behave to get our needs met. As adults, we can say, 'Well, that's one way of looking at it, Dad, but it's not the only way', but as children, if a parent reacts like we've done a bad thing, we've done a bad thing, and that belief stays with us until something forces us to re-examine it, if it ever does. What's your most painful childhood experience? What has it taught you to believe?

We use those beliefs to interpret later experiences

As a teenager, I got to stay up past my bedtime analyzing history with my mother. And whenever I was upset about anything, she would tell me to pull myself together and try harder. I learned that brains were 'in' and emotions were 'out', and that if at first you don't succeed, try harder and never quit. For many years, I was more Mr Spock than Captain Kirk, and I genuinely believed that my worst experiences were those when I acted on my feelings, not my logic. What about those childhood beliefs you've just identified – do they still influence the way you interpret events? (For anyone concerned for my mental health, I've cracked the 'emotions are OK' thing and I'm working really hard on giving up my stubborn refusal to quit even when I'm flogging a dead horse. I'm not there yet but I'm not going to quit until I succeed. Oh dear, maybe I'm not doing as well with that one as I thought.)

And we learn to judge ourselves according to the feedback we get

My British history teacher used to give me A+ and read my essays out to the class, praising my 'delightful prose' (oh, the shame). My European history teacher used to give me C– and suggest, caustically, 'A few more facts and a little less verbiage wouldn't go amiss.' Do you have a behaviour that's admired by some and criticized by others? In judging it, whose views matter most? If you ignored what others think, how would you rate it?

But other people's judgements of us often tell us more about them than us

I bet you learned more in the last example about my history teachers than about me. What about the people who admire and criticize your behaviour? What do their judgements tell you about them?

So we need to learn to reframe

When I lived in Brixton, I saw a poster with two photographs on it – the first was a narrow-angle shot of a black man running along a crowded street with a white policeman running after him; the second was a wide-angle shot showing both the black man and the policeman chasing a third person. It was challenging people who assumed that the black man in the first shot was a criminal, rather than a plain-clothes policeman, and showing them that they were seeing what their prejudice wanted them to see, not what was there.

When is a strength a weakness? The times it doesn't work for you

Are you sceptical about the things I'm saying? Is scepticism a strength or a weakness? When someone has to anticipate negative reactions to their proposals, scepticism can be helpful. When they're responding to radical ideas from team members by dismissing them without consideration, it's probably a weakness. How we judge a characteristic often depends on what our experience of it has been. Have you found scepticism generally helpful or hindering in your experience?

Competence is often a matter of being a round peg in a round hole

I'm not saying we don't have strengths and weaknesses. I'm saying they're just a reflection of how well we fit our operating context. My favourite ever boss was widely acknowledged as a visionary, brilliant strategist and future 'youngest ever' managing director. Yet although he'd been a good enough middle manager to get promoted, there'd been nothing to indicate how exceptional he was to become. In a middle management 'implement other people's strategies' role, he was a round peg in a square hole, but in a director role, he was in his element. What were your best and worst jobs? How did your characteristics fit your best job, and how were they a mismatch in your worst job?

To get our interpretations right, we have to slow down our judging process

Taking a more neutral approach doesn't mean no judging. We need to make judgements to move forward. What worries me is the speed with which we leap to judgement and the fact that, once decided, we lay our judgements down in our subconscious, start to live by them, and forget to take them out for review. And once we've made a judgement, our RAS ensures we see only things that reinforce the rightness of it (the sanity thing again). Given these consequences, it doesn't seem unreasonable to spend a bit more time wondering and exploring before we judge.

And take the time to listen to ourselves

Whatever we're doing, we're doing two things in parallel. Our conscious mind is doing the activity and our subconscious mind is watching us do the activity, making sure our actions are in line with our intention and triggering alarm bells when they aren't. Listening to our alarm bells is the one sure way we have of staying on the right track.

It's not just characteristics that are neutral, it's events

A friend who'd been in the same job for twenty years was made redundant. He said at the time it was the worst experience of his life. Now he says it was the best thing that ever happened to him because it made him stop, take stock of his life, and think about what he really wanted to do. And now he's doing it and he is happier than ever. Did the event go from bad to good? No, his interpretation changed. It's natural to judge events quickly. It gives us closure (what a yuk word), which allows us to move on but which also stops us learning everything the event has to teach us. Have you ever had a bad experience that you later believed had been good for you?

And emotions

Speaking as a former Mr Spock, I'm fascinated when people describe emotions as bad (anger and hurt) or good (happiness and love). Emotions exist to tell us something about an event. Anger, for example, is triggered by someone breaking a rule that we live by or trampling on a value we hold dear. Assuming we've interpreted correctly, anger tells us to put something right that's gone wrong. It's not our emotions that get us into trouble, it's our autopilot responses. Have you ever used anger, in its righteous indignation form, to right a wrong?

And pre-programmes

I have a pre-programme about consultants that says they come into the organization, talk to staff, write up our ideas (the ones our managers wouldn't take seriously when we told them), present them back to our managers (who now take them seriously because they heard them from an expensive suit), and walk off with a small fortune. My autopilot response to this pre-programme involved saying as little as possible to them. Recently, though, I've worked with a number of consultants who've not fit my subconscious expectation. Pre-programmes can be valid at the time we lay them down in our subconscious minds, but times change and we forget to bring them out and check to see whether they still hold up. Do you have a pre-programme about a group of people that you formed years ago? Are you sure it's a true reflection of your current experience of that group?

And even beliefs

Do you believe in the 'do as you would be done by' golden rule? Have you heard George Bernard Shaw's riposte: 'Do not do unto others as you would they should do unto you. Their tastes may not be the same'? As someone who likes to know where I stand with people, it took me a while to realize there are people who'd rather not know – if where they're standing is a bad place. The golden rule can be helpful as a last resort with strangers (a kind of 'if in doubt, do as you would be done by'), but there's no excuse for being in doubt with your staff

– just ask them! Have you ever done as you would be done by and got short shrift?

The difference between the 'push' and 'pull' approaches to managing change

When we're consciously trying to change something (I'm trying to give up interrupting people), we're in push mode, trying hard, working from our conscious mind. When we give up trying to force change and set our intention on being different (being a better listener), and then just observe ourselves in action, we bring our subconscious mind on board and it gently 'pulls' us towards our new intention. Have you ever set your heart on something impossible, not really worked on it, but still found all sorts of help coming your way?

We need to listen to our fears

We live in a world governed by 'feel the fear and do it anyway' sound bites. Well, let's forget the twenty-first-century pop psychology culture for a moment and think about why we have a fear mechanism. Fear is part of our survival instinct, designed to prepare us for fight or flight. It's there to tell us we need to act. If we don't listen consciously to our fears, our subconscious will listen and sabotage our efforts anyway, so we might as well.

And to the people who push our buttons

For years I've been irritated by status-conscious people. It wasn't until I looked back and realized I'd left one job when the organization became open plan and I lost my office and another because some people on my level were regraded to a higher level that I discovered a status-conscious streak I'd denied for years. What irritates you in other people? When do you display the same characteristic? If you don't believe you have it, ask someone you trust whether you have it before you dismiss what I'm saying.

And to our characteristics

Most people focus on their weaknesses and take their strengths for granted. A friend of mine counted listening as a strength, so he listened more than talked in meetings. His boss (who could win an Olympic medal for talking) branded him a poor performer because he didn't make much impact. If my friend had spent more time thinking about how his listening hindered his performance, he might have done something to improve his performance in meetings. What might you do differently if you really listened to your characteristics?

And to the standards we set ourselves

We all have an internal regulator that maintains our standards at the level our subconscious mind thinks is right for us, based on our beliefs about ourselves. What are your standards on tidiness at home? Do you feel you have to tidy up when visitors are due? Or do you always tidy the mess they make as soon as they've gone? If we don't think highly of ourselves, we settle for lower standards than we're capable of, or we push ourselves to achieve perfection – either way, we feel bad about ourselves.

And to the lessons in the experience we create

I had a colleague who believed all men were sexist. Whenever they used the masculine gender as a catch-all for both sexes, she'd tell them to say 'He stroke she'! They made fun of her and she ended up with a negative experience. I preferred to have fun at their expense. I was fond of saying things like 'I'm a man of my word' and watching their reaction – which was comical. By taking their position and exaggerating it until it became funny, I made them think about language without making them feel bad about themselves and in doing so created a different experience of them.

So we can find the beliefs that help and hinder us

Sometimes our beliefs are buried so deep in our subconscious we don't even know we've got them. Looking at our experience can tell us what we believe. Remember that bad habit you failed to give up? If I asked a neutral observer, 'What must my reader believe (about themselves, others, the world at large) to have created the experience of failing to give up that bad habit?', what would they say to me?

We all have an internal cast of characters . . .

I have a friend who's a real monster at work but completely henpecked at home. Another friend runs her own company but turns into a clinging child when her partner is going away on business. And a middle-aged friend who has a 'rebellious teenager' streak who likes to drink twelve pints on a Friday night even though he can't take his drink like he used to. I have a 'repressed child' character who pops out and emotes at people when my feelings are being ignored.

> I guess even the most sceptical of us would accept that different relationships and different situations bring our **different 'sides' to our character**. I like to think of the 'sides' of my character as characters in their own right because it helps me keep a sense of humour and be less self-critical when I do something daft. Each of your cast of characters represents a need that won't go away just because you ignore it and is often associated with a cluster of characteristics you don't use any other time.

Who's in your cast of characters? What provokes one of them to make an appearance? Which ones do you like, and which ones do you try to ignore?

And a dark side that can shed great light on our performance

Whatever you want to call it, we all have a person we're afraid we might be but hope we're not. We have two tactics for dealing with them – if we're conscious of them, we hide them by wearing masks. If we're not conscious of them, we project them on to other people. What characteristics don't you like about yourself? What masks do you wear to cover them up? How do your masks help you? How do they hinder you? Who gets to you in ways they don't get to other people? Which characteristic of yours might you be projecting on to them?

And coping strategies – though some work better than others

How do you cope with criticism? Do you get angry and defensive, or do you listen politely and then ignore it or feel hurt or rush to explain yourself or criticize the person right back or sulk for a few days then do something about it? If you listen, take on board what's useful, ignore the rest, and feel good towards the person doing the criticism, I probably picked the wrong example for you. I'd like to meet you, though, as I've never met anyone who doesn't use a coping strategy for criticism. What kinds of situations do you not like dealing with? What coping strategies do you use? They protect you, but do they have negative effects?

We influence others by acting out our subconscious expectations

My former colleague acted out her subconscious expectation of men being sexist through her attitude and behaviour, and their subconscious responded to what she was giving out. Many organizations have so many rules that they create a subconscious expectation that managers should act like parents and treat their staff like children. As an adult, I don't expect anyone to check whether I've cleaned my teeth, so how come at work we spend so much time checking the work of our staff? The more we act like parents, the more we are acting out our subconscious expectation that our staff will act like children, and the more we will create that subconscious expectation in them. No wonder we don't get excited by the prospect of empowerment programmes. If you empower children, it's all freedom and no responsibility. How do you treat the people you manage? Do you trust them to get on with the task or check up on them all the time?

And they let us – by transferring their power to us

In an organizational hierarchy, people tend to act on their subconscious expectations about authority and power. So, staff expect the manager to know the answers and, in doing so, give away their power and help sustain parent/child relationships.

We also influence by the way we reward and sanction the responses we get

I once knew a woman who could win medals for red-penning reports. Whenever one of her team wrote a report that didn't read well, instead of giving it back to them to rewrite or coaching them, she rewrote it herself. What do you think her team members were learning? What do you do when someone produces a poor-quality piece of work? We don't just reward poor performance, we punish good performance. I know someone who gives all his rush jobs to the person he trusts most. Some reward! What happens in your organization to managers who do good work?

What we focus on expands – so we need to choose carefully

When I wanted my direct reports to improve the way they managed their teams, I started asking them questions about their people management at our reviews for learning. It was amazing how much more they had to report as the months went by. Have you noticed that the better you become at something, the more of it you do? The same thing happens when we focus on our fears. They expand and our subconscious thinks our intention is to avoid the fear becoming a reality.

We can't solve problems with the same beliefs that created them

One of my team had to design a fifteen-day training pro-gramme, which more than 3000 managers would be attending. He said it couldn't be done as with those numbers it would take years. It turned out he was thinking about training people in groups of twelve. I suggested we think about the problem not as training but as event management and we ended up with a conference-style approach that allowed us to train 200 managers at a time in a large venue with lots of facilitators. When was the last time you were stuck? What part of your thinking had to change to allow you to move forward?

And we can't change behaviour until we've changed the beliefs that underpin it

Behaviour is so influenced by beliefs there's no point trying to change behaviour. All that happens when we do is we set up a clash between our conscious mind (which is managing the new behaviour) and our subconscious mind (which is trying to keep us sane by getting us to continue behaving in accordance with our beliefs). Think about a bad habit you've successfully given up. What beliefs had to change before you could give it up?

It's our unquestioned beliefs that lead to autopilot behaviour

Our bad habits tell us a lot about the beliefs we need to question. Think back to that bad habit you're trying to get rid of. What were the underlying beliefs? How long have you held them (how far back does your bad habit go)? How many times during that time have you reviewed them to see if they still hold true?

Asking the right questions transforms behaviour by transforming beliefs

Thinking is simply the process of asking ourselves questions and answering them. The trick to good-quality thinking is asking the right questions. I did a course with some twenty-year-olds. We had one lecture with a different case study every week. The lecturer shouted out the questions and we'd shout back with the answers. Everyone thought they could analyze a case study because they could answer the questions. But the lecturer asked different questions for each case study and the trick to analyzing the case studies was in knowing the right questions to ask – but no one was focusing on learning from his questioning skill. Have you ever argued with someone and been unable to change their mind, only to find that when you stopped arguing and started asking them questions they changed their own mind?

If we want to create positive experiences, we have to sweat the small stuff

People don't judge us on the big things; they judge us on their experience of us. We are much less about our major triumphs and disasters and much more about the person we show ourselves to be in those small moments of choice that happen countless times a day. Sweating the small stuff means thinking of the effect you want to achieve and the consequences of your actions before you make choices so that you make your choices – you don't let your choices make you. What makes you decide whether you admire someone?

And get off autopilot on to manual

Just because our brains like being on autopilot doesn't mean we should let them. People aren't machines. Press the key on the computer keyboard that says T, and T is what you'll get every time. Speak to the same person in the same way two days running and, if their mood or circumstances are different, you will get a different response on day two than you got on day one. Does this tie in with your experience?